Finding Happiness Pedal by Pedal

Amy Hudson

Finding Happiness Pedal by Pedal

Pegasus

PEGASUS PAPERBACK

© Copyright 2024
Amy Hudson

A CIP catalogue record for this title is available from the British Library.

ISBN 978-1-80468-074-2

This is a work of nonfiction. No names have been changed, no characters
invented, no events fabricated.

*Pegasus is an imprint of
Pegasus Elliot Mackenzie Publishers Ltd.*

www.pegasuspublishers.com

First Published in 2024

**Pegasus
Sheraton House Castle Park
Cambridge England**

Printed & Bound in Great Britain

Dedication

To my husband Kyle for being there through the darkest
moments and always believing in me.

What Is This All About?

If you've ever slipped on a puddle of ice in winter and almost fallen over, then you've experienced a split second of anxiety. That feeling where your heart drops to your stomach, you let out a little 'woah' and your breath gets taken away for a second. A moment later, you steady yourself and maybe have a little laugh, feeling glad that you didn't fall over and embarrass yourself. That feeling you have for a tiny part of your day doesn't stop for someone with anxiety. Imagine that feeling. Now imagine it all day. Imagine it all day, every day. That is what my anxiety has felt like in the past and can occasionally still feel like today. I say 'my anxiety' because I'm not claiming to be an expert on anxiety; everyone's experience is different.

When I first set out writing this book, my head was creating its own ice puddles in the form of intrusive thoughts that seemed impossible to avoid. I didn't get the feeling of relief for not falling over because I did fall over every time an anxiety-provoking thought slapped me in the face. (A bit like when I fell off my bike on tree sap on a commute to work last week; let's just say wet conditions and tree sap make for an excellent ice rink.) Some days were better than others, with smaller, non-icy puddles. But other days, there was a whole ice rink and I didn't have ice skates. On the worst days, I fell and couldn't get back up. Even though there were many times when I didn't feel like getting back up and didn't want to, I did. I never gave up; there was something within me that knew life would get better again. Along the way, I discovered a passion for cycling, including dancing on top of hills to celebrate a climb and yippeeeing back down them again. Cycling has truly changed my life; along with support from friends, family and counselling, it brought my real smile back. And now here I am, sat in my lounge (in Lycra, having just got back from my commute and not having the energy to shower right now, sweat stench alert), reading over and editing this book, in the hope that it might get published one day, feeling in a much better mental place.

With help along the way from cycling, I can honestly say I'm happy; I'm not one hundred percent free of anxiety; I don't think anyone is. I'm not one hundred percent rid of my eating disorder; they tend to stick around for a while. But I'm working on it. I'm not always dancing and yipeeeing and I still go through low times. But on the whole, I'm happy, I'm calm and I feel like nothing will send me back to where I was before because I always have the option to get out on my bike, something I'm so grateful for.

The ice has cleared and if it comes back, I've got shoes with better grip, or should I say I've got cleats to clip into my bike and pedal the negative thoughts away.

No matter how bad your anxiety is, no matter what worries are there, remember that you're not what your head says. No matter how low you feel, how worthless or useless, how much you don't want to be here, you are worthy and you do deserve to be here. From all that I have been through in my mind, I always tell myself not to lose hope. Things can get better; you are stronger than you think and one day, you will be happier. If, like me, you struggle with anxiety, intrusive thoughts or an eating disorder, even though it may seem impossible to believe, your thoughts and worries are not reality; this is something that took a long time for me to learn! They're the worst possible case scenario created by your head, which someone without anxiety would probably never even consider a possibility. My head is a master of worse-case scenarios; it's like it wants me to live in a constant thriller or action movie; everything that could go wrong is brought into play. My mind could create a drama series about a carrot if it wanted to. Let's take going on a dog walk before work; on an anxious day, my mind might think the following; 'what happens if you drop your house key, then you can't get back in the house, then you can't get to work, your phone is in the house so you can't let work know, then everyone will wonder where you are, then you might lose your job' so then I'm walking the dog with my house key in my pocket like it's a million-pound note. Or Kyle being five minutes late home from work, 'What if he's had a car crash and he's really injured and he's in hospital and I don't get to say goodbye to him, or what if he's had a car crash and it's his fault and his van is written off and we can't afford to get him a new one and his insurance goes up and then he'll have to get the bus to work which will cost so much money…' Kyle gets home fine as always and wonders why I greet him with such relief! Luckily, although I have these thoughts, I've come to accept that it's the way my mind thinks and, on the whole, I can ignore them; it's a work in progress. But when I was really struggling, back when COVID hit and I was struggling at work, I couldn't ignore my worried thoughts.

People have said to me, "Amy, you've got nothing to worry about, honestly I would tell you if you did," and I used to think they were lying to me to make me feel better. I couldn't believe that something bad wasn't going to happen. In my head, I had no positive future, I was a bad person and I deserved things to go wrong. I can't count the number of times my husband Kyle has reassured me that my worries will never come true. Although his reassurance was somewhat comforting, at times, I was trapped so deeply in my thoughts that however hard I tried, I couldn't believe him.

Things do and can get better. This is coming from someone who has beaten an eating disorder (well, I say beaten; it still lurks around, but it's under control). This is coming from someone who has beaten intrusive thoughts (yes, these are defo beaten, as beaten as my knick-knacked legs – or even better, Kyle's after a hilly bike ride). This is coming from someone who had constant thoughts they were a bad person and was certain something bad was going to happen. Someone who has had sleepless nights due to worries that have never materialised. Someone who has had to sing songs to drown out distressing thoughts. Someone who once cried on the kitchen floor curled up in a foetal-like ball because the thoughts all got too much. Someone who at one time planned not to be here anymore. Someone who still gets anxious and may always get anxious, but someone who will not be beaten by anxiety.

It makes me sad and somewhat embarrassed to remember back to the summer of 2020. This was when I was at my worst; I was crying whilst painting the garden fence because I was convinced I had done something wrong at work and was going to get sacked from my job as a mental health nurse. I feel embarrassed about the thoughts that consumed my mind because I now know they were completely irrational. I feel robbed of the moments of reality that I lost to the irrational moments happening in my mind. I lost so many moments living in my own head instead of living in the real world. It's only when I look back that I recognise how quickly my mind can become unwell and how unwell I got. But in those moments of illness, what was happening in my head was all real to me and I truly believed I was a bad person. It even got to the point that I was convinced I was going to get put in prison; now, anyone who knows me will tell you I'm the least likely person to be put in prison. In reality, there is no way I would break the law; I haven't even gone as far as trying a cigarette, I always stick to the speed limit in my car and once I mistakenly didn't pay for a chocolate bar that got lost under a mound of bags in the trolley at Aldi, so I ran back in to pay for it, no lawbreaker over here!

Hopefully, this book will shine a glimmer of hope for you. Hopefully, it will help you to see that even if you suffer from mental illness, joy can still be found in the darkest of places and you can do things that you never thought you would be able to. Hopefully, it will help more people to talk and not feel embarrassed and if no good comes from it, it has been quite therapeutic for me to write (also very scary because I haven't spoken openly about the intrusive thoughts much!).

Everyone's experience of mental illness is different and I'm not an expert in any way, but if you take one thing from this book, know that you are not alone and you are an important part of the world, so never give up. If you're reading this book as someone without any experience of mental health illness, I hope you enjoy the insight and at the very least, I hope everyone that reads this book gives cycling a go because it really is life-changing (we're more than just annoying objects on the road, sorry if we slow your journey down a little!).

I know how hard reading can be when your mind is constantly thinking, so if you're struggling with anxiety or intrusive thoughts right now, I hope you will be able to concentrate on the words in this book. Take it a sentence or a page at a time if that works better. One word a day is an achievement.

Little mental health tip: When small shoots of stillness enter your mind, enjoy them. Before you know it, those shoots will grow into meadows. Never give up hope that your meadow will grow.

An Introduction to Me

Describe yourself in three words is the classic interview question; it sounds simple, but it's really hard to answer honestly. I really don't know what three words I would pick. I'm a woman who loves being outdoors, animals, cooking, eating curries, cafe stops on rides, chai lattes and hot chocolates, dancing on top of hills and yippeeeing back down them on my bike, seeing how far I can cycle, spending time with family and friends, reading, laughing, walking, dogs, but most of all cycling. I'd like to say I'm kind. I care a lot about how other people feel and have a tendency to want to make sure everyone is okay, but at other times, I can be a right grump to live with and want to shut away from the world, disguised by a smile when I'm out and about. I'm determined, hard-working and driven and I put pressure on myself to do well. From the outside, I'm happy, living my best life, carefree. But on the inside, I struggle from time to time and I worry a lot; I go through cycles of feeling amazing to feeling like there's no point in life. Some days, I wake up and the misty mind is there; it creates a low fuzz over everything, life moves slower, things feel harder and motivation is lacking. On other days, I wake up and I have a sunshine mind; everything feels right and I want to take on the world, dishing out the jokes and being my silly self. I've struggled with my eating and sometimes still stress about it; I can fall back into old habits from time to time and feel like I have to do a certain amount of exercise to justify the cafe stops (something I'm currently working on) or get stressed out if I don't do as much cycling as planned. My mental health is in a much better place than when I started writing this book, but I'm not hundred percent there with it; I don't know if I ever will be, but that's okay because, on the whole, I love life and you don't appreciate happiness as much if you never go through hard times.

In the depths of it, my anxiety and intrusive thoughts took away who I was, so I didn't know myself anymore. People would be talking to me and my eyes would be looking at them but not really seeing them, my ears taking in the words, but my mind not able to process them. I suppose it's a bit like when you've been on a really long ride and you haven't fuelled yourself properly; you come home feeling a little out of it or, worst case, you bonk (that's not a good thing in the cycling world! It's where you run out of energy and you basically can't feel your legs; it usually results in a taxi home or emergency call to a friend or family member to beg for a lift home. Luckily, I haven't had to do this so far. I was recently saved by a corner shop where I whacked down three samosas and a magnum ice cream to get me home, but from what I've heard, it's not nice at all!). It felt like living just a few seconds behind the rest of the world; no one else would notice, but I felt behind and below everyone else.

When I was really struggling, I kept to my morning routine, which I still do now: alarm at six a.m., get up, change, take the dog out without my phone, no distractions. I used to look at the people I walked past or at cars who drove past me, joggers who heavily breathed their way along, wishing that I could have a bit of their carefree air. I wish I could walk along with the lightness they seemed to have.

When I drove to the food shop each week, I would look around at the other cars (whilst stopped in traffic, don't worry, I was safe on the road!), thinking about all the lives driving past me that I knew nothing about. I felt glad about my irrelevance and the fact that they knew nothing about the failure of a person driving the car next to them, but at the same time, I wondered what those people did. What lives do they lead? Maybe, they're like me, they appear happy, but really, they aren't. The truth is we don't really know much about the people that pass us by every day. Millions of lives, with billions of details, that will only ever be known by a tiny few.

The problem with the "describe yourself in three words" question is how do we describe something as complex as a human in only three words? Do we answer with what we really think, or do we try to think about what the people around us want us to be?

Sometimes, I feel like I'm a different version of myself, depending on who I'm with; I shapeshift to fit in with the expectations of those around me. I'm sure everyone does it a little bit; you might be more jokey with your friends and quieter when at work, you might act calm and collected when you're on a walk with your extended family but be the most irritable person ever when you're at home. At the end of the day, we all want to be accepted, right? But do we ever stop to think about the version of ourselves that we truly want to be? The version where no one around us influences how we are? Being afraid to be your real self might prevent you from going for things and from enjoying life. Accepting who I am and being my true self is something I am working on. Cycling has definitely brought out the most true version of myself; it's where I feel like I can be me, I don't overthink what I'm saying, happiness just invades and I don't care what people think when I'm letting my inner child out on the bike, having a laugh and dancing around, because I'm in such a great mood (most of the time, I can't say riding in the pouring rain and wind you'll find me in high spirits) that I'm not trying to act in a way to please anyone else but myself. I feel like cycling brings back the child in me, the carefree side, where anything is possible and everything is to be explored. We're all discovering things about ourselves every day and that means as we grow, we have the power to change who we are and want to be; that's freeing. I never used to cycle, but I can't imagine my life without it now. You never know when you're going to find the thing that helps everything else in life slot into place, but when it comes, roll with it; you'll know when you find it. Whether it's sport, music, cooking, or cycling, if it brings a sense of home, makes your soul shine and gives you a reason to get up in the morning, then it's the right thing for you. Keep searching for what makes you happy because when you find it, life becomes amazing, trust me.

So...I haven't answered the question. Maybe you can read this book and pick your own three words to describe me. After all, the question is not of benefit to me; it's for the person asking the question.

So, who actually am I?

Well, the thing is, you don't know me personally and you probably never will (you might know a bit about me if you follow my social media; I'm in shock that I got any sort of following. I didn't have my insta account or YouTube when I started writing this book). I could be the girl who walks past you on your way to work; I could be the man who sat next to you on the train yesterday; I could be the shop assistant who told you to wait in line for the changing rooms; your child's school teacher, your manager or the person that was in your way at the shop when you were trying to reach the pasta. Basically, I could be anyone, everyone, from the strangers who pass you by each day to the people you have known for years who are susceptible to mental illness. Even those who say they don't believe in mental illness, yes, these people still exist. Anyone can struggle with anxiety or intrusive thoughts, but most of the time, we never know about it, or we don't know the real depth of it. Maybe we don't ask how people *really* are on a deep level because we are too scared about what they might say. Or maybe people are too scared to delve into the real traumas of mental illness past the common phrases of "feeling a little low", "I've been anxious", or "a bit stressed" due to fear of judgment. Maybe people try to tell us how they feel, but we don't really listen; we don't want to be burdened with the problems of others when we have our own to deal with. We don't know what we're meant to say; we're worried about saying the wrong thing and we don't want our family members to be struggling, so we ignore it, not wanting to make the problem any worse. We block it out because we can't deal with how upset we feel about someone we love not coping. We can't cope if they're not coping, so we pretend that everything is okay. We can't cope with the idea that we're not coping, so we pretend to cope. Expectations on what life 'should' be like make us scared to admit when it's not going to plan, embarrassed that we can't deal with something, shamed by our own minds when, in fact, if we spoke out about our struggles, life can get better and there's nothing to feel embarrassed or ashamed about.

I don't know if it's just me, but I sometimes get the impression that the actual gut-wrenching pain and suffering that comes with mental illness isn't quite accepted, understood, or freely spoken about yet. The more we have open and honest conversations about mental illness and realise that it doesn't make you any less of a person, hopefully, the more understanding and acceptance there'll be. Unfortunately, you can't just 'snap out of it', 'think rationally' or 'let it go' when you're struggling and the more people who understand that, the better we will be able to recover, speak openly and feel accepted. I still feel embarrassed about the thoughts I used to have and sometimes still have lurching in the back of my mind; I know they're totally irrational, but that doesn't make it any easier. I shouldn't feel embarrassed about it; I didn't choose to have intrusive thoughts and I didn't choose to become unwell, but I did feel extremely embarrassed and shameful about it all like I should have been able to 'think normally' and 'be fine'. I've wasted time getting angry about the way my head works and there've been times when I wished I could take my brain out and leave it out for a while, not wanting to deal with the thoughts flying around in there. But I can't take my brain out or switch it off, so I've learnt ways to deal with it and sometimes I just have to get on with what my mind throws at me and enjoy the good times.

In a slightly bigger nutshell than usual, I'm Amy, a wife, daughter, sister, niece and friend to a very select bunch of people who can put up with me! I'm twenty-seven years old at the moment (I started writing this book in small chunks when I was twenty-four, as a distraction from the torment in my mind), but with the rate I am doing this, if this book ever makes it anywhere, I will probably be thirty-five by the time you are reading this. I live with my husband Kyle, who I've roped into cycling and who's stood by me through my difficult times, a bit like I've stood by him whilst he curses up hills on long rides; I conveniently miss out the elevation level detail when letting him know about the route (if I told him the amount of hills before we set off I would probably be going solo, so best to leave him with an element of surprise)! In some ways, we're opposites; he's chilled and I'm not; he loves football and I couldn't care less…but somehow, we work and I wouldn't be where I am now without him. We moved in together after two years as a couple and got married after three, getting our big scruffy rescue dog, Chester, pretty much as soon as we got our first house. For me, a house isn't a home without a dog, although I sometimes have second thoughts, like this morning when I got home to the sofa pillows on the floor, toilet roll ripped up all over the bathroom and the kitchen bin emptied out, I also have some slight sense of regret when I'm woken to the sound of him retching to be sick on the pale-coloured carpet. But all his faults aside, Chester has been like a therapy dog for me and I've got so much love for his furry face and butter wouldn't melt eyes, so I wouldn't change a thing about him (although maybe if he was a tad smaller, I'd be able to take him on the bike in one of those pull-along trailers!).

My family are everything and although we argue like every family does, my mum, dad and two younger sisters are always there for each other; family are a massive part of my life.

I tend to avoid nights out; it's safe to say you're unlikely to find party animal and me in the same sentence; sticky floors and waiting for a taxi in the cold aren't really my scene. Early to bed and early to rise is my preference. Once I'm awake, I'm on with my day and you don't see me sitting down relaxing much, which some say is anxiety-driven; I say it's productive and I like to get things done... some things I'm not willing to change!

I wish I could give you some exciting stories about my life so far, but my life hasn't really been too unusual. I was born on 29/03/1996 to amazing parents who were counting down the days until I arrived. I was the first of three girls; my poor dad has always been outnumbered by women; even our dogs, hamsters and guinea pigs were female! My dad shed a tear when he first saw me, or so I'm told. Mum proudly placed me in my brand-new car seat that'd been waiting for weeks to bring me home. Dad videoed my tired but proud mum carrying me down the drive home (a memory we have to re-live with a family video on every birthday), where a brand-new cot was set up ready for me by the side of their bed and a freshly painted Winnie the Pooh bedroom waited patiently for me for when I was ready (maybe being exposed to Eeyor from a young age is where my love of donkeys has come from!). I grew up in a lovely house with my parents, two younger sisters and an array of various pets along the way; we could have set up a small pet shop with the amount of animals we had! For some reason, our goldfish always had the most unusual names; I seem to remember a Plankton and Hamish at one point...

We all got on well as far as families go. The guinea pigs and dog had a troubled relationship and there were a few incidents where my sisters and I would 'wrestle' on the trampoline and may have come out with the occasional bite mark...but that's normal, right?

ifs, just going with the flow and not getting worked up about tiny things going wrong. But then I come to my senses; I have no clue what 'laid-back' people are feeling inside; we can all put a mask on to the outside world whilst being tormented on the inside. Once, a colleague told me that they wished they could be as calm as me in stressful situations; little did they know the turmoil going on inside my head, all unleashed when I got home each night. I feel so sorry for Kyle when I think back to my worst days; I would literally get home and be mute, all my talking energy taken, with nothing left to even ask him how his day was or have a conversation about something boring like the weather, I must have been so difficult to live with and I still feel guilty about it. When I was younger, if my parents went out, even though my grandparents would babysit, I wouldn't be able to sleep until I heard their car pull onto the drive. I'd be convinced they were going to have an accident and might not come home. I'd always ask my mum what time she thought they'd be back and then the clock-watching would begin. As soon as it went a minute past the time they were meant to be home, the worries would start: they've had a car crash…one of them has had a heart attack…they've left us…what happens if they die…who would look after us…I also used to have an obsessional worry that we were going to get burgled or that someone was going to kidnap me, despite the fact that we had never been burgled, nor had anyone we knew. But every knock on the door filled me with a sense of danger. I have to laugh when I remember one time my friend and

I were home alone (we were more than old enough to be) and someone knocked at the door; she also shared my fear of burglars, so us two together wasn't a good combination. We convinced ourselves it was a kidnapper or something and decided to make an escape on scooters down the side of my house and scooted to her house around the corner as fast as we could…only to see the so-called kidnapper a little while later, who was, in fact, a St Johns Ambulance volunteer asking for donations. I'm not as bad as I used to be, but I know if any intruders come along, I'll whip straight off on my bike!

Being the eldest child, I didn't have an older sister to look up to and tell me what was fashionable or give me tips on how not to get picked on. Who knew that the brand of plastic bag you took your PE kit to school in had such an influence on your social status? Combine this with the fact that I didn't develop any breasts until I was about sixteen and it's not a great recipe for popularity. I remember one moment in the PE changing rooms when I overheard two of the 'popular' girls saying, "Look what she's wearing under her shirt; she's so flat-chested." this comment meant that no boy would ever find me attractive and I would have to get a boob-job. I remember going shopping with my mum and begging her to let me have padded bras even though I had nothing to put in them. I was so desperate to be like the other girls in my year. I used to google how to make your boobs grow bigger – according to Google eating more fatty foods and plumping cream, don't ask! Luckily, I now accept my small boobs, which did eventually grow, so the boob job is no longer on my to-do list; I have much better things to spend my money on...bikes. It's so sad that at such a young age, the way we look has such a massive impact on how we're treated by the people around us.

I should also mention that when I was sixteen and starting to struggle, my younger sister was diagnosed with anorexia. She was so unwell that she had to go to hospital for eight months. I was seventeen, she was fourteen and my other younger sister was eleven. The house was broken. I lost the sister I used to know to the depths of anorexia way before she went into hospital, but her physically not being at home anymore made the loss feel much more real. It felt like our close, happy family was being torn apart. I spent most weeknights at my boyfriends to try and distract myself and weekends were spent visiting her. I don't want to delve too much into this; that's her story to tell if she wants to, but it's something that impacted the whole family and it's what led me to become a mental health nurse, one decision I would definitely change if I had a time machine.

So, what happened to my mental health? I do and have always put pressure on myself to do well. I don't know where this innate sense of needing to achieve comes from, but it must just be part of the way my brain is wired. My parents always taught me to 'just try your best', but in my head, anything below an A/A* wasn't good enough. There's no doubt that A levels are pressurised for everyone; you're trying to figure out what you want to do, maintain or achieve some form of social status or acceptance, flirt with the guy you've fancied for over a year, revise for exams, deal with the hormones flying around everywhere and on top of all that…learn how to drive, no wonder insurance is so much more expensive for younger people! Combine everything that's going on with an innate sense of pressure to do well and a tendency to doubt your ability and I think it's fair to say the stress of A-levels felt doubled. (Even now, writing this book, my self-doubt prevails: thoughts filling my mind that it's a waste of time because no one will want to read it).

I remember being very low at times, anxious a lot of the time and determined to do well all the time. I worried about my future and didn't know what I wanted from life. I started to have frequent panic attacks and whenever I was at school, all I wanted to do was go home. I don't know why I wanted to go home, but I just did; it's a hard feeling to describe and one that I still get now. I just get an uncomfortable feeling that I can't shake and a longing to go home. It's usually when I'm in a social situation (never when I'm cycling socially, though) that I just become disinterested in the conversation around me and no matter how much I try to be interested, my mind and body having none of it, I can't feel 'right' until I'm in the car on the way back home. It annoys me because it stops me from enjoying social moments; there's no rush or need to go home, but it feels like getting home is the most important thing at that moment.

I was good at masking my worries and my friends and teachers wouldn't have known anything was wrong unless I told them. I'm good at pretending to be okay. The down moods, which I still experience now but not as often, make the world seem misty and like I'm disconnected from everyone around me. It feels like nothing really matters, yet at the same time, the smallest of things stress me out. It's a very confusing mindset to experience. But it's all too easy to mask with a smile that turns to tears or just results in me being a complete arse-hole to everyone behind closed doors, with no energy left to fake a smile at home. I remember the night it all came out to my mum. My younger sister, Bethan, had just been admitted to the hospital; I was lying in bed, feeling helpless against the thing that had taken my sister away. I started to feel really down, coupled with being stressed out about exams and ashamed for feeling low. 'I have a nice family, friends and a lovely home; what reason do I have to be down? I should be happy; I'm so ungrateful. I don't deserve to be happy if I'm going to waste my life feeling like this'. This thought of shame and embarrassment only filled my low moods further. I somehow got stuck in a deep rut of not feeling good enough, stressing myself out so much about exams that I started to question the point of life; if all I'm doing is feeling stressed and exams, then what is the point? I started to think more and more about the meaning of life and came to the conclusion that it was pointless, drained with endless longing for my sister to be okay but knowing that nothing I could do would cure her, sick with worry about whether she would ever get better, whether my mum was okay as I could see how upset she was no matter how much she tried to wear a happy mask. In my mind, there was no reason for me to feel so low. I had everything I needed in life, but no matter what I did, I couldn't shake the feeling. As I lay in bed one night, tears streaming, probably with depressing music on in my headphones to really add to the mood, I shouted my mum into my room and told her everything. Saying those words to my mum, 'I sometimes feel like I don't want to be here anymore' and that I had been hurting myself, was one of the most awful things I have ever had to do and I hate to think about it, even eleven years later it still makes me shiver.

Mum encouraged me to go to the GP and sixteen-year-old me nervously told the doctor that I had been struggling, again, tears streaming down my face; we'll have enough to fill a swimming pool soon. The doctor handed me some thin, rough blue paper tissue to wipe my tears (the kind that any primary school injury would be met with 'put some wet paper tissue on it'), told me that I needed to speak with my school nurse and sent me on my way with a leaflet about depression and anxiety. There was no way in hell I was going to talk to anyone at school about this. (On a side note, I know and have seen so many amazing GPs, so I don't want to discredit the amazing work they do). I went home with Mum and told her that I would be okay and not to worry about me because I would get through it. Just telling my mum was a big release for me and feeling like I had someone on my side helped a little. I was so determined with my grades that I put all my focus into that. I pulled myself along and came out of sixth form with high grades, which I collected in disbelief as the self-doubter in me told me that I must have failed every exam. And then off I went to uni, but I still had overwhelming feelings of anxiety, put a lot of pressure on myself and at times felt very disconnected from those around me, almost like I was walking around in my own little bubble, still in the world but somehow not hundred percent in it.

During my A levels, the pressure I put on myself to get good grades meant I was constantly revising, which was meticulously planned out to the minute with colour-coded timetables. I wouldn't let myself watch TV until I'd done a certain amount of hours of work; what a crazy teenage life I lived! I was constantly being asked about what I wanted to do with my life. How is a seventeen-year-old with no real-life experience meant to know what they want to do for the rest of their life? Decisions are something I have always found difficult, mainly because I think of every possible outcome and go over these thousands of times, eventually concluding that whatever choice I make will end in something going wrong! Choosing paint colours and furniture for our first house was a nightmare, which, in the end, I left mainly for Kyle to make the final decisions on and to be honest, there have been a few rooms completely repainted due to changing my mind. When I was hit by a car whilst cycling (more on that later), choosing a replacement bike was painful for everyone involved! Researching about all the options, changing my mind, questioning my decision, to be honest, the main thing I go for when choosing a bike is the colour (sorry cycling enthusiasts) it's got to look good, of course, I'm picky about the gears too, they're important for getting the cod loins (aka legs, yes, I call them cod loins, more on that later) up the climbs! I left sixth form equipped with my A levels, a whole load of anxiety and my mind set on being a mental health nurse, wanting to help as many people as I could.

To sum me up, I'm just one person in a massive world, in an even more massive galaxy, who is trying her best at things. There is no manual for life. Although I struggle with life at times, on the whole, life is good now and I'll always find a way to keep going through any roadblocks that come up.

Be Yourself

I'm trying to be myself.
But who is me?

How can I be me?
In a world that won't let me be.

I'm not sure how to be the real me
When everyone else is only being what they want others
to see.

Little mental health tip: Start your day by saying something positive, such as "Today is going to be a good day; I can tackle anything that comes my way". Even if you don't believe it, saying it can help.

A Bit About the Eating Disorder

Unfortunately, whilst studying at university, I developed an eating disorder (ED); how ironic! My anxiety fuelled mind, coupled with the stress of worrying about my career choice and not being able to switch off from the people I saw struggling when on placements in numerous mental health teams, made the perfect environment for an eating disorder to nestle its way into my anxious mind; needing every assignment to be a first or I'm a failure, needing to be early to every lecture or I would miss something really important, walking fast to and from the train station with my bag tightly under my arm in case someone tried to mug me, yes the burglar/kidnapper thoughts still prevailed. I think it came about as a way of coping; focusing on food and exercise gave me an escape from the stress I was feeling and a sense of control. I started off by going to the gym because I wanted to get fitter; I got obsessed with having abs and would look in the mirror multiple times a day, picking apart what my tummy looked like, feeling disgusted with what I saw in the mirror. Desperate to look toned, get thinner, be pretty whilst feeling so ugly because of having acne that I didn't want to look at myself. It started to spiral by the week: counting calories, weighing food, weighing myself monthly, weekly and then daily. It got worse and worse until I was weighing out lettuce. I needed to know exactly how many calories I was having, or it would lead to a meltdown. I remember one low point of my life was crying about eating crumpets, chucking them in the bin and then battling with my mind, half telling me I needed to get something else to eat, half praising me for not eating. But when you're in the depth of an eating disorder, you lose your sense of self; my mind was totally controlled by 'the eating disorder', "don't eat that", "you're ugly", "you need to burn that off", constantly thinking about food, ruled by a voice in my head that got stronger and stronger, no matter how much exercise I did, how many calories I cut out, it wasn't good enough, stricter rules would be created and more would be cut out. My rational voice that told me I should get something to eat, that it's okay to eat, was getting smaller and smaller.

Food and exercise are something I still have a tricky relationship with from time to time, but after eight years of dealing with it, I'm in the best place I've been and cycling has been a massive help. There are times the ED thoughts creep in, but I remind myself that I never want to go back there and keep repeating, 'If I can't fuel it, I don't do it.' I'm never going to get far with my cycling if I don't have enough energy.

The ED had a cunning way of slowly invading my mind and bedding itself in so deeply that it was stuck like superglue before I even recognised it was there. It became so ingrained that it felt almost impossible to get rid of. I learnt from helping my sister to separate the ED from myself, but at times, it was hard to distinguish between my own thoughts and the ED's thoughts because they became so loud, they drowned out anything else going on in my head.

Before admitting I had a problem, deep down, I knew I was struggling and I was so angry at myself; 'I've seen what an eating disorder does to those around you, so how could I get one? Surely, I wouldn't let myself become ill after seeing everything my sister went through? How am I going to be a mental health nurse if I'm not right myself? How can I help people with eating disorders if I've got one myself?' It took me a long time after noticing the ED to pluck up the courage to talk about it. Although I noticed it during uni, it might have started to sneak in earlier than this; at age fifteen, I can remember that I didn't allow myself to eat the Mars bar that a friendly lady on my paper round used to leave me on her doorstep unless I'd been swimming. I can remember in sixth form making an effort to eat 'healthy' and never allowing myself to have fish and chips on a Friday lunchtime like my friends did and always saying no if sweets or chocolate were offered my way. At the time, I didn't recognise this as anything other than being 'healthy', the latest trend to follow, but looking back, maybe this was a warning sign.

There are some key ingredients that might have helped the ED grow inside my mind:

My lovely friend anxiety; the eating disorder masked this for a while and maybe it was easier to hide behind it and allow the anxiety to take second place for a while

Being a sensitive one, I take things too personally at times and tend to dwell on them; I used to be really in tune with the comments people made about my body or what I ate.

I am naturally a perfectionist; when you apply perfectionism to trying to eat 'healthily' in a world full of mixed messages about what healthy is, a logistical food nightmare begins. Perfectionism is actually a well-known predisposing factor for developing an eating disorder cited in lots of research and evident in lots of the young people I worked with when I was a nurse.

I've never really liked my body (or if you want the proper terminology – negative body image); comments I heard about my body at school did not help and neither did the awful acne that the joys of puberty brought!

Social media was full of bodies and diets; the constant pictures I was seeing of toned bodies, six packs, thigh gaps and clear skin created an image of perfection that I wanted to achieve.

I think I started to pay more attention to what I was eating when my sister was discharged from the hospital. She was on a meal plan to put weight on and I started comparing my eating to that. I figured out that I was eating more than her, so I thought: 'Surely I must be putting weight on?' Little thoughts started to creep in. First, they were about trying to be a little healthier, then came doing more exercise...wanting to get toned...needing to get toned... and finally...having to get toned. In the end, I got obsessed with everything body-related: counting calories in, calories out and a strict diet where fatty, sugary foods were hell and lettuce were heaven. If I ate a forbidden food, guilt would cripple me. Feeling hungry meant I was going in the right direction. Fullness was forbidden. The gym was my second home, trainers my go-to shoes, the scales my partner in crime, stepper apps a new companion and coldness an unwanted but accommodated guest. Thoughts of food would both control and overwhelm my mind. I'd throw a snack in the bin and then instantly wish I could eat it. My mind is in an endless battle against itself. I would be constantly planning what the next meal or snack would be. Calculating how many calories I would need to burn at the gym to eat 'bad' food whilst making sure I left enough room in my daily allowance for dinner with my family. I'd lie in bed at night planning what would be on my menu the next day, which was such a waste of time because apart from dinner cooked by my mum with my beady eyes watching over it, I pretty much ate the same every day. I was an absolute stress pot whenever I was invited out for a meal with my friends, pre-reading the menu ten times over and calculating what would have the least calories. Crying in the toilet after eating no-cheese, gluten-free pizza. Nights out were no fun when you weren't allowed to drink alcohol, birthdays boring when you couldn't eat cake and meals out torture when you had to watch everyone else eat puddings that you wished you could have a bite of. That's the weird thing: I was desperate to be able to eat what everyone else was eating; as people took a bite of cake, I would imagine the taste, wishing I could take a piece too, an invisible internal battle going on in my mind constantly. But I knew if I took a piece of cake, the next few hours, my head would be unbearable and I'd feel like I wanted to break out of my own skin, so it wasn't worth it. I was also worried that if I did eat a slice of cake, I wouldn't be able to stop. My life was controlled by rules made by the ED; 'don't eat that you'll get fat', 'You need to burn this many calories at the gym', 'Don't drink alcohol. It's bad for you, 'weigh out your food then you'll know exactly what's in it', 'don't eat past this time', 'you can eat that if you do this exercise'. The worst part of it was that I would lie to people about what I had eaten or what exercise I'd done. Weight became the focus of my life and it left me in a constantly bad mood at home because I used up my energy on a fake smile when I was out and about. I wasn't meant to have scales; my mum and Kyle said it wouldn't be good for me. They were right, but I snuck to Tesco and bought some anyway, obsessed with a number. The eating disorder turned me into a completely idiotic child at times: tantrums when I was told I needed to eat my dinner, throwing food in the bin and saying no when asked to eat; I was basically a toddler. Looking back, I'm so embarrassed about how I acted: arguing over something as silly as a snack, convincing myself that people were lying to me when they told me I wasn't fat. It saddens me that the scales were the judge of my worth and no amount of hugs, love or reassurance could comfort me as much as the number on the scales going down could. But that's the reality of eating disorders that's so often misunderstood. It's not just being stubborn, attention seeking, or a 'phase'; it's mental torment that I wish no one ever has to experience.

I'm so lucky that I didn't carry on spiralling in the direction I was going. When I finally admitted that I was struggling, my mum was amazing and already knew what was happening, so she was ready to help me. I went to the GP, but unfortunately, I didn't meet the criteria for the eating disorder team because my weight wasn't low enough. This could easily have turned into a new target for me to get to, but I didn't let it be. I had some therapy, which was okay; it gave me a push in the right direction and I made a promise to myself and my family not to let this beat me. I unfollowed all the unhelpful, stick-thin image social media accounts and instead followed positive ones that encouraged eating enough rather than starving yourself. I used the determined part of my personality to work against the eating disorder rather than with it. It took A LOT of hard work and determination. At times, it felt like I was fighting against myself, but it's all been worth it.

I do still struggle with my eating at times and I have to be careful that I'm cycling for enjoyment and not to 'burn off' calories, particularly during stressful times. But that's a story for a different time. Cycling has helped me unbelievable amounts with this side of things because if I don't fuel it, I can't do it, so I'm constantly getting the food in and bringing the cafe stops my way! I discovered a chai latte along the way and boy, was I missing out; if you've not tried one, I urge you to; it's like Christmas and warmth in a cup, sweet nectar as I like to say and its D to the E licious.

Little mental health tip: Be your own biggest fan, cheer yourself on and be proud of yourself for all the challenges you get through.

Remember, it's a miracle that you're here and no matter what your mind says, you are good enough.

Little Pep Talks

Throughout this year and, to be honest, the past three, I've had to give myself little pep talks to keep going through hard times. Sometimes, I have to be tough on myself to make sure I eat enough or to prevent myself from getting pulled in by anxiety. Realistically, it was the ED and anxiety that I was being tough on; it will throw any excuse your way to stop you from getting better, so you have to be alert and watch for it sneaking in.

For example, the ED would and still occasionally does tell me things like 'Don't eat that', 'you're lazy' and 'You can't eat that unless you burn off this amount', so a meeting between the ED and me has to take place in my head, a bit like I'm psyching myself up for a boxing match, ready to tackle whatever my opponent throws my way.

The ED can disagree with all it wants, but I don't give up. You have to keep your motivation up. An example of what I might say to myself in these moments would be: "That's the eating disorder talking and you've spent far too much of your life listening to it, but now you don't have to. Remember all the reasons why you are fighting this, life will be better without the eating disorder", or now it's more like "You are not going back there, don't even think about it, you've come too far, now eat that cake and enjoy it!". It's kind of like having a stubborn child living in your head that won't stop whining until you give it what it wants or if you are able to ignore it, it will get bored of being ignored and quiet down.

I give myself pep talks when I'm out cycling; when the route seems to be never-ending and the legs feel heavy, I find the motivation to keep going from the inside. I can either ride along cursing the road or force out a smile and focus on the good things, like the meal I'll have when I'm home, the fact that I'm fortunate enough to have a bike, that I have time to ride, that there's an open road ahead of me and I have the freedom to ride for however long I want to. It's so easy to get sucked into the negatives and miss the positives that are all around us.

Little mental health tip: Look in the mirror and instead of picking apart what you look like, focus on all that your body does for you. What are you grateful for about your body?

For me, it's my legs for being able to cycle, my eyes for being able to see the gorgeous countryside views, my ears for being able to hear the birds singing as I pedal along and, of course, my taste buds for all the delicious snacks I eat along the way (not forgetting the chai lattes).

More than Looks

One thing that has helped me in recovery from the eating disorder is reminding myself that I am more than what I look like (it's not easy to think this way and there are times when I don't believe it, but it helps). It sounds simple, but your body is so much more than what it looks like. In the world we currently live in, it seems that what our body looks like has become way too important. Humans have survived in a world where there was no such thing as make-up, spot cover-up, hair gel, aftershave/perfume (although we all appreciate that on sweaty bike rides), fake nails or false tan. We wouldn't be here today otherwise, but it somehow seems that society/the current way of life has led some of us to believe that we are not good enough the way we are. It's so sad that we can feel so uncomfortable and unhappy with how we look naturally that we feel a need to try and physically change what we look like or feel too self-conscious to join in and have a good time.

Let's take the focus away from looks for a moment and imagine that every human looked the same. The same body shape, same nose, ears, eyes, hair, everything. There would be no comparison to how each other looks. Then would we be happier? Or would the world be boring? It's what makes us unique that makes the world and each of us amazing. You are beautiful just the way you are. It's amazing that you look the way you do; no one else does (unless you're an identical twin, of course!); no one can take what you look like away from you.

What's amazing about everyone's body? There are so many things that go unnoticed because we're all too busy judging each other and ourselves for our looks. Your body is amazing. Nose for smelling, eyes to see beauty, ears to hear music, legs that can walk, cycle, run...the list goes on. The best thing? Our body does what it does and what it looks like doesn't influence that. Having severe acne doesn't stop a person from being able to see vibrant colours or smell beautiful flowers, but the way a person is made to feel about their acne by other people or by their own inner critic can prevent them from enjoying the vibrant colours or beautiful smells because the doubts about their looks take over and become intrusive. Having acne when I was in uni (which I think was a trigger for the eating disorder; I felt like my face was ugly and I couldn't do anything about it, but I could do something about what my body looked like) and again after coming off the pill from age twenty-three to twenty-six is something I've found really hard. I'd look in the mirror each morning and absolutely hate what I saw. Cover-up makeup costs a fortune and even more time to put on; I'd never leave the house without it on. Luckily, my spots have gone now (time and stopping using all products and just washing my face with fragrance-free soap worked for me), but I do have a face full of scars and I still feel very self-conscious without makeup on. I wish I could get up, whack my hair up, strap my helmet on, tighten up my cycling shoes, clip in and pedal off. But at the minute, there's a whole make-up routine that has to happen first because I can't bear the thought of anyone seeing me without make-up on. I'll openly admit I look in the mirror and I feel ugly. I'm not comfortable with my skin, I'm uncomfortable and there are loads of things I want to change when I look in the mirror: dark circles under my eyes, my wonky bottom teeth, slightly whiter teeth, shinier hair, thicker hair, spot scars...the list could go on. But I remind myself that most people are so worried about what they look like they aren't going to notice your insecurities. It's like when someone says, 'I've got this massive spot' and you only notice it after they've pointed it out. I listened to the 'Happy Place' podcast by Fearne Cotton the other day and it was said that we should look in the mirror and tell ourselves we love what we see, even if we don't believe it, because the more we do it, the more we can start to accept the way we look. So, this is what I'm doing at the moment and it feels weird, but it's a nice weird.

In cycling, like in all sports, it's easy to compare body shape. I get so many comments, "Ohh, you're skinny. You'll be good at climbing", "I wish I was as light as you to get up that climb." I don't really mind too much when people comment on my body shape. I've always been built like a stick with twig arms, but there is a little eating disorder devil inside me that clings on to these 'skinny' remarks and fuels my mind to say 'Stay skinny'. A Lycra jersey isn't the most flattering, it really does bare all and I think there can be pressure in cycling to be light; I've heard the term 'race weight' or 'climbing weight' thrown around even in local club rides, I know that in the pro-teams leading up to a big event like the Tour De France (which is on at the moment and I'm LOVING it, stage one the Yates brothers battling it out to the end was a great watch!) diet and get down to their race weight, but they have nutritionists, it's all planned out and I hope that they are fuelling themselves enough during the event and afterwards. If my mind starts running away with weight and cycling, I bring myself down a few pegs – I'm not a pro rider in any sense, so keep on cycling and stop being silly! Even on local club rides, the conversation often turns to diet and watts (how much power you put out when riding) and it's not uncommon to be asked how much you weigh; in my mind, it doesn't matter what you weigh, anyone can ride a bike, there is no weight or diet rule, just sit on the saddle, spin your legs and enjoy it, you don't have to wear Lycra, wear whatever the hell you want, I recently went out on a ride in a T-shirt and it felt great, although I did miss the pockets on my jersey for snacks!

We have created an importance on looks and we have the power to uncreate it. Let's celebrate what our body does instead of what our body looks like. Healthy doesn't mean thin; we are all naturally different shapes, so embrace your body shape.

Little mental health tip: Life doesn't need to follow a set path; you can change direction whenever you want. When you take the leap to choose happiness, life becomes freer and worries become less.

So do the things you have to do with a smile, say yes to the things that feel right, no to the things that feel wrong and don't be scared to make changes if you think it'll make your life happier. It's never too late to try something new.

The Short-Lived Nursing Career

I went into my nursing degree full of excitement; the idea of helping people and feeling like I had an understanding in some way made me think that this would be the right job for me. But the problem was I couldn't switch off. I kind of knew after my first nursing placement, where I spent the whole hour drive home crying, that maybe my career choice wasn't the right one. But because I was so determined not to give up. I hadn't done a placement in the eating disorder area (which is where I wanted to work), but I stuck out the degree; a bucket load of tears later (I think we have half a swimming pool full now), I got my qualification and headed out to be a nurse, working with people who had eating disorders. My career as a nurse wasn't a happy one; I wouldn't be able to sleep because I'd be worrying about the people I was supporting, caring so much that my own health got pushed to the side. The worries started to creep in and gradually overtake me; I'd start thinking 'what if'…and my mind would run wild with all the things that could go wrong and could be my fault. It was in the depths of COVID whilst working in a child and adolescent community eating disorder team when things got really bad or, as I like to say, things hit the pan. I didn't notice it in myself at first, or more likely, I didn't want to admit I was struggling. But slowly, my anxiety was getting the better of me. Working from home every day, I was alone with my thoughts. Appointments with a young person would end and I'd sit in my office overthinking what I'd said, worrying if I'd missed something important they'd said or that I might have made things worse rather than better. The team I was in was really supportive; I wasn't alone and I wasn't solely responsible, but my mind made me feel like I was. Ever since hearing 'coroner's court' in a lecture in uni, my mind clung to it and scared me with it most days I was at work. I have a tendency to self-doubt, which is not what you want when you're in a caring role. Once I get an idea in my head, it's really hard to get it out of there. Don't get me wrong, that has its perks, too; my overthinking and determination mean that cycling challenge ideas keep coming and I don't tend to give up easily! It got to a point where I wasn't sleeping properly; I'd wake up every morning with an upset stomach, dreading opening my laptop and live for the weekends, which for the last few months of my job were no fun at all because my mind wouldn't let me rest. I remember doing strength and conditioning workouts on FaceTime with my sister some evenings after work (these were the times when households weren't allowed to mix) and I couldn't focus on the exercises because I was starting to get consumed with intrusive thoughts. I don't know how it happened or over what time period; it's all still a bit of a blur to look back on.

thought. At the dinner table, the first time I blurted it out, Kyle suggested that I stop work for a while; he told me he thought I was unwell and this time, I had to listen. I knew he was right, although I couldn't really understand this at the time because everything was a blur between reality and intrusive thoughts. I didn't really take in the fact that I was leaving my job, but I was so terrified of making a mistake and the whole prison thing it came as a relief. I didn't have to wake up feeling sick with dread of going to work any more. But, of course, the thoughts didn't immediately stop; it took months to get back to anywhere near how I was before the intrusive thoughts invaded my conscience. Once they did eventually fade, I was plagued with feelings of inadequacy, failure and worthlessness that I couldn't hack. I was so ashamed that I'd spent four years studying at university to become a mental health nurse and only spent three years being a nurse.

When I reflect on it, although there are things I miss about it and I loved learning about mental health, I never really enjoyed the job. It didn't suit my overthinking mind and we only have one life, so you need a job that you enjoy or, at the very least, can switch off from. I know I helped some people, which is the positive I can take from it. I work in finance now, which is a complete change, but it suits me so much better; I can't harm numbers, haha! I still have a sense of shame around this, but I'm slowly learning to accept what happened and that life doesn't always follow the path you think it will. You can plan life out, but there's never any guarantee it will go to plan.

I still find it hard to think back to that time; I was even reluctant to write about it. I'm scared people will read this and think I'm weird or look at me in a different way. I'd hate to be treated any differently because someone thinks that my mental health defines who I am; it doesn't. But then again, it kind of does, too, because I think if I didn't go through that, then I wouldn't have the never-give-up mindset I have when I'm on long or hard bike rides. I haven't done any amazing rides compared to a lot of people, but I have aims to do more and more endurance and when I did Everesting last year for a mental health charity (cycling up and down the same hill repetitively until you've cycled the equivalent of the height of Everest) it was knowing that I got through the 'I'm going to prison time' that helped me keep going because no challenge I've done on the bike has been harder than the mental torment that caused.

Little mental health tip: Comparison is the thief of joy (so I heard in the Happy Place podcast, Fearne Cotton, one of my favourite podcasts); there will always be someone 'better 'or who seems to have 'more' but that doesn't make you any less of a person. So, let's celebrate the achievements of others and focus on finding our own sense of happiness. Let's boost each other up instead of putting each other and ourselves down.

Discovering Cycling

It was in my last few months working as a nurse that I discovered cycling. It was a time when I needed something to take my mind away from what was happening in my head. And now I've discovered it, I'm not letting it go.

Kyle bought me a bike and without that gift, I honestly don't think I would be as happy as I am today. It was a Carrera from Halfords, hidden in the spare bedroom that needed decorating, a little gem against the plaster-less wall, waiting to be ridden. I got straight out of my dressing gown and into casual clothes and did a little test ride around our street, like a kid on Christmas morning. I'd never ridden a bike with drop handlebars on, so it took a bit of getting used to. It wasn't an expensive carbon road bike or anything like that; you don't need an expensive bike to cycle; it got me outside, exploring the countryside and led me on the route to finding happiness again. I will admit I now do ride a more expensive beast, as I like to call it, but I saved up to do this and I must admit I feel a little bit of guilt when I think about people who can't afford to buy a bike, my overthinking mind is always finding a way to take the enjoyment away, but I know there are some things out of my control, solving world poverty and everyone being able to ride an expensive bike are some of them. I didn't have any padded cycling shorts or Lycra and I had no clue what cleats were; my bike and helmet were all I needed to start with. I'd ridden a bike before, but not for a long time; my dad used to take us on bike rides at weekends or after school in the summer when we were younger, something me and my sisters would try any excuse to worm our way out of. The ride always involved a pub stop and Dad would always try to encourage me to try a Dandelion and Burdock drink; I eventually did and decided to stick to lemonade. I remember one ride we went on; Molly, my youngest sister, had not long been born, so Dad took me and Bethan out. I was six and Bethan was three, in a seat on the back of my dad's bike. We were coming down a hill and I didn't realise we were turning right at the bottom, not the usual route home, but Dad was going to take us to the park to give my mum more time alone with Molly, worried about being left behind I slammed on my brakes and turned right, but skidded and flew across the concrete, all my chickenpox which I was recovering from, scraping off and causing my T-shirt to cover in blood, maybe that's what put me off cycling for a while! We came back home with more rather than less stress for my mum. I cried as she gave me a bath and washed the cuts.

I went through a phase of cycling to school for about a year because it was quicker than walking. But I had no desire to cycle other than when I was forced to. I remember cycling home from school and worrying about what the other people in my year would think; I wasn't in any 'in-group' to begin with, but I added a bike and rucksack into the mix and it's not a recipe for popularity.

This time, cycling was different. I had chosen to pick up the bike and I wanted to ride; I had nothing else that was making me feel anything. I started off by going out on rides with my dad two Sundays a month; these rides gave me a reason to keep going in my job for a little while and gave me something to look forward to. My dad's always enjoyed going out on bike rides at weekends on his Dawes Galaxy touring bike (which I currently have in my garage and used to commute to work on before working from home) and has been cycling since he was thirteen years old. He's since upgraded to a Genesis Tour de Foix, in which he shows off the built-in dynamo lights (as you pedal, the lights get charged) to anyone who will listen, but I will admit I am slightly jealous of them. He's not a fast cyclist; he just likes to potter along and enjoy the views. He could probably go faster if he wanted to, but he doesn't and that's the great thing about cycling; there are so many different ways to ride, but the most important thing to me is enjoyment.

Those rides every other Sunday were like a form of therapy for me. No. They were therapy for me. I had counselling and a small stint of trying medication (it didn't agree with me/ I didn't give it enough time to work), but nothing compared to what cycling does for my mind. Dad always planned the routes using a paper map (he has now got a Garmin after discovering their existence but still prefers his map). We didn't have a bike sat-nav to pre-plan the route and I didn't use Strava, two things I now never ride without! We'd spend all day cycling two Sundays a month, rolling through the Peak District, peaceful country lanes, with grass growing down the middles of some of them, gravel to dodge on sharp corners, challenging hills with fifteen to twenty percent gradients, my dad joking as he always does, bringing his Trangia for soup and hot drinks at lunchtime no matter what the temperature and carrying far more than needed for a day out, including whole tins of soup, packs of nuts, a ground-sheet for sitting on while we ate lunch, there were no cafe stops to be had when out cycling with my dad, although he occasionally got tempted by a pint in a pub once they were open after COVID! After I'd left my job and things were at their worst, we increased our cycling to most weekends and slowly, slowly, a pedal at a time, a bit of me started to come back. Bike rides were the only thing I looked forward to; they were what kept me going. Don't get me wrong, counselling helped a lot, too and Kyle was amazing; without him, I wouldn't have gotten through it, but the cycling just gave me a different feeling, something that words aren't advanced enough to explain. I didn't need to talk about anything or think about anything while I was on the bike; I could just be, enjoy the views and feel subdued by the nature around me. There were lots of rides when I was really struggling that got ruined by anxiety thoughts that would still be repeating over and over in my mind, almost in rhythm to the speed I was cycling; these were the days that were the hardest. But even though the ride didn't necessarily help on days like this, turning the peddles gave me something else to focus on and being in nature created a level of calmness that I couldn't find anywhere else. Being in the fresh air with the thoughts was better than being at home with them. I soon discovered the addictive nature of cycling and the desire to see how far I could go started to grow.

It's two years on from when I first started cycling as I sit here writing this. Starting with a fifty-mile ride (Dad didn't break me in lightly) that felt like it lasted forever and like I'd run two marathons (let's just say Sunday dinner was devoured post-ride), we were soon riding seventy, eighty, ninety and then hundred miles, which was celebrated with a drink in a pub in Repton on the way home and my dad jumping in the air and clicking his heels together – he's where I get my dancing habits from! I'm never more content than when I'm out cycling, free-wheeling down long hills, crawling up steep climbs, the wind blowing against me, rain soaking through my clothes, sun burning down on my face, nature making me aware that it's much bigger than me, but reminding me that I'm part of it, I'm living and it's exhilarating. I don't really mind what the weather is doing; as long as I've got my raincoat and enough layers to be warm, I'm happy.

I heard nothing but the ticking of the chain on my bike, the wind blowing past my ears, cattle and sheep, occasional cars or motorbikes, tractors, a combine harvester, gravel crunching under my wheels and birds calling out from the bushes. Being surrounded by views of nature, tones of green roll around me from the fields endlessly in all directions, trees sporadically spreading throughout the landscape. I notice the stones in the road, moss growing on the trees, birds flying in the sky, all the little things that would be missed if I was driving. It brought me into the moment and out of my mind.

I always set out on long bike rides determined to complete the miles, knowing that unless I get injured, cutting the route short is not an option. The feeling of success when I get home after a long day is incomparable to any other achievement. I feel whole, my happiness levels topped up, my muscles aching but in a good way and my mind full of the views I've experienced. And then there's that blissful feeling of having a shower, putting on comfy clothes and digging into a dinner post-ride (a curry is usually my favourite option).

Like anything in life, there are people who ride much further than I do and people who ride much faster. There are people who ride much less and much slower, but everyone who rides a bike, no matter how fast or how far, what bike or what kit, is a cyclist. I'm happy in my lane; I go at my own pace and I enjoy it. I do it to feel free and alive and gain a sense of achievement from it. I'm making the most of the beauty outside my doorstep. Of course, me being me, I have some aims for the future in endurance, but for now, I'm seeing where it takes me and rolling with it.

When I left my job, I felt like a failure. Not knowing what I wanted to do career-wise at the age of twenty-five was not part of my life plan. I felt like all my friends were better than me; they earned more than me and I felt as though I would never get back to where I was before. I didn't want to start from scratch again. I had the motivation to find a new job, but at the same time, I had no idea what I wanted to do. I took time off and taught swimming for a while, something I've done every weekend since I was seventeen, but that wasn't enough for me. I loved it, but I needed something that made my mind think more and my skin wasn't loving the daily chlorine dose! I eventually found myself at an interview for a trainee finance role and somehow, I got the job. A bit of a change from nursing, but it suits my perfectionist mind and I'm content with it. I'm not going to lie and say I absolutely love my job, but it's interesting enough for me. I don't feel stressed and I can ride my bike carefree; that's what matters. As long as I can ride my bike and have enough money to pay the bills, then I'm happy. Don't get me wrong, I'm naturally an aim-high sort of person, but since leaving my role as a nurse, I don't ever want to let myself get to that point of break-down again and the way to do that is to try not to pressure myself, which for the moment is working.

Although cycling is usually my happy place and I want to spend as much time as possible on the bike, I can't lie; there are times when I compare myself to others. Comparison is a natural part of being a human and it's not a surprise that it thrives in the sporting environment. Endurance is what I want to focus on because it's what I love the most, but this year I gave racing a little go. I'm willing to try everything and we need more women on start lines, so I thought, why not give it a go and encourage other women to do the same? I'm somehow part of a women's race team; last year, I did a few races and managed to get my category three licence (you start at cat four and move up by getting points). But I find myself constantly thinking, 'I shouldn't be part of this race team', 'I'm not good enough', 'The other girls don't like me.' as you can probably tell by now, my mind has a habit of putting myself down. I find the races quite stressful, building them up in my mind to far more than what they are. I wish I had the confidence of the other girls in the team, but I have visions of myself falling off a corner and ruining my bike or breaking my arm. Breaking something is my worst nightmare because I don't know how I'd cope without being able to escape through riding or exercise. As others whip around the corners, I'm on the breaks, anxiety-mind taking over. I did a crit race last week (this is where you ride around a track outside for a set time; first over the line is the winner). I cried on the way there and asked Kyle to turn the car around, but he said he knew I would feel better for doing it and he was right; once I got on the track after the first few laps, my mind settled and I started to enjoy it. I finished the race (I came fourth!) smiling and with a post-race buzz lasting a few hours, feeling super proud of myself for challenging my anxiety and not letting it stop me. I immediately entered the race for the following week. But the day it came around, I was in an awful mood and I knew that I wouldn't be able to fight the anxiety feeling as well as I had done last week. So, I swapped the race for a club ride. My anxiety took over and my head wasn't in it. It's just local races, nothing big. It doesn't matter if I come last (which I have), but I put so much pressure on myself on the inside that sometimes it's not worth forcing myself to do it. Other times, it is worth doing it because I prove to myself that I can do what my mind tells me I can't, but realistically, I want cycling to stay as something I enjoy, not a pressure. I'm still annoyed at myself for not racing last week (I paid for my entry and could have bought a few mid-ride chai lattes with that!). I felt so guilty all day the next day I cried (again! I'm not usually a crier) because I felt as though I let the team down by choosing to go on a club ride instead of going to a crit race. I don't know what was worse, the pre-race anxiety or the non-start guilt. But you can't change what's already happened and next time, I'll use the fact that I felt guilty last time to urge myself to do the race. So, I've decided to keep up the racing until the end of this year because I'm part of the team, it's a good bit of cardio and I do enjoy it once I'm there...but next year, my racing will come to an end. I'm all about cycling for enjoyment and I find that most on long-distance rides. Bring on lots more Audax (Long-distance cycling association, more about that later) rides and hopefully some ultra-distance events in the future. If there's one thing I've learnt from my experience of 'break-down', it's to do what feels right for you, don't be afraid to try new things, but if you try it and you don't enjoy it, then don't carry on doing it. Don't worry about what other people think and try not to compare yourself because the person living your life is you. Compare yourself to a past version of yourself, aim for a better future version and be proud of your current self for putting your happiness first.

Little mental health tip: Every day, remind yourself to stop. Stop rushing around and take three long, deep breaths. Focus on the cool air going in through your nose and coming out slightly warmer. Notice calmness comes over your body.

Anxiety AKA the Moment Thief

If you have anxiety, I imagine you get what I mean when I say that my mind doesn't seem to have an off switch. My mind enjoys thinking of the worst-case scenario and running with it at hundred miles an hour until I've convinced myself I'm going to prison. Luckily, I've managed to create a dimmer switch. I can't turn the anxious thoughts off, but I can respond differently to them and most of the time, I'm able to prevent myself from being blinded. But I won't lie; there are occasions when the switch gets stuck on for a while and I don't know how to turn it off. I get wrapped up in the thoughts and for moments or sometimes days, I'm a walking ball of anxiety.

There are often days when I feel like my mind is like a scrambled egg. Not the nice, buttery, golden-goodness type. The stodgy, dry, been cooked for too long type. On the scrambled days, I don't know what I'm feeling or thinking and I can't make up my mind about anything. Don't ask me to choose what we're watching on tele or what we're having for dinner because you'll be waiting until tomorrow. On these days, I'm just not with it.

One morning, whilst walking the dog, just after leaving my nursing job, thoughts flying around all over the place, I slipped on an ice puddle and almost fell over. For a second, I was brought out of my head and into reality. I was actually glad that I slipped because it meant that I had no choice but to focus on my balance; slipping gave me a tiny bit of relief from the thoughts in my head. In that small moment, I was grateful to be brought away from the turbulence in my head and into reality. It was at that moment that I realised how bad things had gotten and I recognised what I knew deep down: anxiety is a feeling designed to protect us from things like slipping over, but the anxiety and intrusive thoughts that I had been having weren't protecting me, they were ruining me. It was shortly after this walk that the "I'm not going to prison, am I?" Was blurted out to Kyle at the dinner table

Being a perfectionist and hating mistakes, it isn't surprising that my anxiety really took a turn for the worse while working as a nurse. Before I qualified as a student nurse, I questioned whether it was the right choice for me. But I refused to give up. I wanted to help people and I didn't want to fail, so changing my mind wasn't an option. I stuck it out; as a student nurse, you spend fifty percent of your time in uni and the other fifty percent in placements. Let's just say I looked forward to the uni time. I had numerous placements in dementia wards, acute wards, drug and alcohol teams, community mental health teams and adolescent mental health wards. I can't say I enjoyed my placements, but I did find comfort in knowing I'd helped people and I was determined to work towards helping people with eating disorders. When working in an acute ward (a specialist mental health ward for people who are unwell and would be unsafe living at home, usually unsafe to themselves rather than anyone else) for elderly people, I always remember having a conversation with a lovely lady who was one of the patients. She was struggling with depression and one day, on the ward, I sat with her for a while in her little private bedroom, helping her organise her belongings into her drawers. I said to her that I didn't know what she had been through but reassured her that things could get better and I encouraged her to try and focus on the small things that bring her joy. Knowing that this had helped me before without being able to tell her this, she said to me, "You have a wise mind for such a young soul" and that comment has always stuck with me. When she was discharged from the hospital and able to go home, she held my hand and said thank you for bringing me some hope. She had a little tear in her eye as she squeezed my hand. My heart felt warm and I realised that the smallest of comments can make a world of difference. Another memory I have from placement is from the female acute ward. This was my first placement and I was nineteen at the time; there was a young girl who was only eighteen on the ward and she was struggling with depression and self-harm. One day on the ward, I could see that she was distressed; I went to sit with her and taught her how to crochet because I find that the constant movement of your hands when crocheting helps with sitting still and calming down when feeling stressed or anxious. The girl seemed so pleased just to have something to focus on and said, "Thank you for noticing me." it was moments like this that kept me going, knowing that I had helped someone.

On the days when my mind was completely consumed by intrusive thoughts, my body was in the room, but my mind wasn't. I can recall a meal out with Kyle and his Grandparents. We went to a local pub, the same pub Kyle and I went to on our second date back when I was still a student. They specialise in homemade pies and when I first met Kyle, I wasn't able to eat a pie because of the eating disorder, but in a strange way, the intrusive thoughts I experienced helped me to eat properly again because the amount of calories I was eating no longer mattered, I was more worried about being put in prison or worse. So, this time, I ate a whole pie with buttery mash and minted gravy and I didn't feel guilty about it (until the next day); every cloud has a silver lining, I guess. Before the meal, I had considered cancelling; the last thing I felt like doing was socialising, especially with having to sit outside in the cold because of COVID-19. But I didn't let myself cancel because I knew that'd lead to a downward spiral of cancellations and then feeling guilty for cancelling and wishing I had gone and then having to make up for it somehow and feeling like a failure. Are you starting to see how my mind works? At the meal, the conversation was going on around me and I didn't feel like part of it. Joining in was an effort; understanding what the point of the conversation was even more of an effort. I've felt like this so many times before. Thoughts that evaded my mind made it hard to concentrate on the present; my head felt cloudy and, in a weird way, my eyes sensitive to the light. All I could do was focus on the physical table or the menu in front of me, trying to stay in the present and just get through the meal. I noticed how happy Kyle looked chatting to his grandparents about the cruise they were about to go on and about how his building job was going; I felt guilty that I didn't make him as happy as other people did. I didn't have a reason to go home, but I just wanted to go there. Kyle's Grandparents didn't have a clue how I was feeling. To them, I was smiling and chatting and joining in just fine; I'm a master at pretending to be okay. But underneath eyesight, my leg was tapping, my fingers clenching and unclenching, my thighs tensing, my eyes looking to my watch or to my phone, counting up how much sleep I would get that night (getting eight hours is a must) or ruminating over what I had done wrong. My mind told me that I looked ugly, I had said the wrong thing and my laugh sounded stupid. We got in the car to go home and like many times before, I said to Kyle, "So glad that's over" and he said, "I know you didn't really enjoy that, did you?". The strange thing is I did enjoy it a bit; I still liked to go out for meals and see people, just in small amounts. Small doses of people were great, but lengthy meetups were not so great; it's like my mind could only cope with so much socialising.

Things I Say to Myself to Help with Anxiety

- Everything right now is okay
- Things that have already happened can't be changed; things you're worried might happen probably won't happen, so focus on now
- Ninety-nine percent of your worries never come true
- Stop, three deep breaths, as slowly as you can, continue
- All the worries in your head are made up by you; make up some happy thoughts instead
- Stop with the 'what if it goes wrong?' and start 'what if it goes right?'
- Nothing bad is going to happen
- Close your eyes and imagine the calmest place you can; stay there for a few minutes
- One day, you're not going to be here anymore, so all your worries are irrelevant; enjoy yourself!

These things don't miraculously make the anxiety vanish, but they help.

Little mental health tip: When you're out and about today, look up and smile; it spreads a little happiness and we all need a bit of that.

Accept

Accepting how you feel in the moment when it's a bad moment is hard. But once you can accept how you feel, the feelings become less painful and more manageable.

Feeling anxious and worried is awful and debilitating, but I often like to remind myself that the feeling comes from within me; I have the power to feel a different way. Although in moments of awfulness, I feel like nothing I can do will make it go away, it always does go away eventually. I used to get very annoyed about feeling anxious, saying to myself, "You're so stupid" and "Why can't you just be normal?" but my frustration only made it worse. So now, I've learnt to let it be; I know it will pass. Instead of fighting it, being angry with it or magnifying it with unhelpful coping mechanisms, I simply let it be. It's like when you're on a bike ride and you hear that awful puncture sound, look down and yep, the tyre is flat. You can either get really annoyed about it, wishing you had seen whatever it was, swearing, or, in some instances, even resort to kicking your bike. Kyle did do that near the end of a four hundred km ride when we got a puncture in the middle of the night and the pump wasn't working…I think the Ribble came off better than his toe; we do look back and laugh about this now. It was an awful time to get a puncture, to be fair to Kyle and it was his longest ever ride, so he was feeling a little knick-knacked: one am in the morning, dark and looking like it could rain, eight miles from the end of the ride and about forty minutes added on because of this little mishap, luckily some helpful fellow cyclists stopped to help out, turned out their pump didn't work either! The third cyclist that stopped had a working pump, got it going and we all rode the eight miles to the finish together. It turned out well in the end and we bought a new pump when we got home! The other way to react to a puncture is to remain calm (a great way to make sure no toe injuries are incurred); no matter what you think or how you react, the puncture is still there and still needs to be fixed. No matter how angry I get about my anxiety, it's still there; it goes quicker when I do the things that help, like reminding myself it passes, doing a little less, eating right and moving my body and I definitely fix a puncture quicker when I'm calm compared to when I get worked up about it. So now, when anxiety or low mood pays a visit, I let the feelings flow along, I accept that it's here, I accept that this will be a hard few weeks and I feel safe (not always, but I try to) in the knowledge that they won't be there forever. I wait for happiness and I wait for calmness and it's always worth the wait. When you get a day without anxiety, it's amazing. Just the other day at home, I had a whole day of no anxiety, a calm day of cleaning, going on a little bike ride to meet a friend for a chai latte (of course) and cooking dinner. No worries came into my mind, no racing heart and no random outburst of tears. My mind is starting to become clear again and I'm starting to get me back, whoever that is. When you get a day without anxiety, after living with it for days, weeks or months, it's the best day ever and you really appreciate just being able to do your day without worry.

Little mental health tip: Sometimes you need to stop and notice what's around you. Come out of your head and into the moment. Take some time each day to focus on what's around you — what colours can you see, what can you smell, what can you hear?

The List

I can clearly remember one of my really bad days when my mind wouldn't stop. I was trying to be strong and distract myself, pacing around the house; Kyle was at work, which added to my guilt; I was a failure, I wasn't contributing and worst of all, as my head told me, I could be going to prison. I kept saying to myself, 'I AM NOT A BAD PERSON.' I wanted to shout it to stop my thoughts, but I was also scared of being taken to a mental health hospital, so I didn't. Instead, I wrote myself the following list, which is still on the note's app on my phone:

- I am a good person
- I've not harmed anyone
- Kyle will always love me
- I can get through anything that's thrown at me
- I've only ever acted with the intention to help people
- I'm not a bad person
- Kyle and my family will love me no matter what; even if I was a bad person, they would still love me
- I deserve to be happy
- I've not broken any laws intentionally

- Mistakes are okay
- The world is not ending
- Consider every opportunity to have a good time
- I can't control what has already happened or what might happen
- I have never intended to do anything wrong
- I can get through anything; I have so much to be happy about and not worry about

Looking back at that list now, I let out a little laugh when I read, 'I haven't broken any laws intentionally.' I don't know what laws I thought I'd mistakenly broken! At least I can laugh at it now. I'm sitting here on my sofa, Chester curdled up on the rug, looking at me with his big cute eyes and a shaggy mound of fur, waiting patiently for his walk and I feel content. My mind isn't racing; I have clearness, something that, at the time I wrote this list, was impossible to imagine. I realise how great it is to be able to sit here without any horrible thoughts, something that I took for granted before the 'I'm going to prison' episode occurred. I won't take it for granted anymore. Next time I'm stressing over some crumbs on the kitchen worktop or a pile of washing to do, I'll remind myself of how nice the clear mind is and not to stress about the little things. I've always had thoughts in my head: I don't know what it's like to think of nothing; is that even possible? But when you've had moments where it doesn't feel like your mind is yours any more, having clearness is an amazing feeling, something that is so simple that we don't notice how good the good things are until we don't have them anymore. The fact I get worked up about crumbs on the worktop is a good sign; when I was struggling, I didn't notice the crumbs any more, maybe that should be one of my warning signs – doesn't moan about crumbs on the kitchen worktop, let's have a mental health check!

Little mental health tip: You never get any days back, so make the most of each and every one.

North Coast Five Hundred
Round One

Trip details:

Day one – Inverness to Loch Carron – sixty-five miles

Day two – Lochcarron to Loch Maree – seventy-two miles

Day three – Loch Maree to Ullapool – sixty-five miles

Day four – Ullapool to Kylesku – fifty-nine miles

Day five – Kylesku to Tongue – sixty-five miles

Day six – Tongue to Keiss – seventy-two miles

Day seven – Keiss to Golspie – sixty-three miles

Day eight – Golspie to Inverness – sixty miles

My dad and I enjoyed our weekend rides so much that while we were on a ride one day, whilst sitting outside a petrol station in Bakewell with a milkshake, we started talking about a cycling trip. My dad mentioned that he'd heard about the North Coast five hundred (NC500), a five-hundred-mile ride around the highlands of Scotland, as we sipped more excitedly on our milkshakes and an idea was formed, a few months later and a lot more milkshakes down our gullets, we were on our way. I must say I did have to upgrade my Carrera for this trip as she definitely wouldn't have coped with the weight of the panniers; I hadn't discovered the art of packing light at this point! I upgraded to a Focus Atlas, which was a great bike for this trip, but it turned out it was slightly too big for me, so Kyle ended up with this bike. Once I got home, he also got the cycling bug, but had to sell the bike to a cyclist in London as it was also too big for Kyle. It was a rookie mistake not checking our frame sizes properly!

The NC500 was my first big cycling trip and I was full of excitement and no anxiety. When I'm with my dad, I feel worry-free and that everything will be okay…because he's the responsible one! We spent eight days cycling the coast of Scotland, five hundred twenty miles of pure exhilaration. I could probably write another book just about that trip. The views were amazing, the fresh air immense and the miles hard but exciting. I loved every second; even when I got blown off my bike four times by extreme wind, I was still in good spirits. Yes, that actually happened…on day five of the trip, there was a fifty-mph crosswind between Durness and Tongue, so any attempt to cycle ended up with me in a sheep fence. We stopped in Durness for lunch and sheltered behind a village shop. I was genuinely concerned that we wouldn't make it to Tongue; I wasn't strong enough to fight the wind and I'd never experienced anything like it. We had no choice but to keep on going, but after I was blown off for the fourth time whilst battling more of a headwind, making it up the West side of Loch Eriboll, Dad turned around to see me lying on the road, panniers luckily protecting the bike from any scratches, we reluctantly decided to walk for about four miles until we crossed the Loch and a tailwind awaited. Camper vans passed us with concerned-looking couples; motorbikes stopped to tell us it gets worse when you cross the loch as it becomes a strong crosswind; they were going back to where they came from and re-trying tomorrow. We had no choice but to keep going and I was worried we wouldn't make it, especially with the fear that it would get worse. A kind couple in a camper van pulled up alongside us and asked us where we were going; it turned out they were also going to Tongue, and they offered to take our Panniers for us; we handed them over and suddenly, it became much easier, to fight the headwind. We slowly got back on, pedalling carefully, passing sheltering sheep, a random peacock and a cafe that shone a smiler of hot chocolate hope, which was soon slashed when the closed sign came into sight. We had no choice but to walk again when we crossed the Loch, if you can call it walking, leaning towards the wind and trying to stay upright! But once we were over and changed direction, we had an amazing tailwind all the way to Tongue, where our wind-beaten red faces were looked at in either awe or utter shock by the Scottish landlord and our bags were waiting for us; what a relief as I had convinced myself that the camper van couple might just drive off never to be seen again. We both opted for a three-course meal that night!

I'm happiest when outdoors exploring and I find nature so calming. But that wind showed me how powerless we are compared to the force of nature; I was anything but calm when being blown at full force into a sheep's fence! I wasn't calling out "Hello, sheepy" that day! I was more focused on not becoming entangled with a sheep as the wind blew me in their direction. A gust of wind was strong enough to blow me over, so I dread to think what it's like in the winter; the locals told us that the wind we experienced was nothing compared to usual!

There's never a shortage of camper vans on the NC500 route, ideal when you are in trouble but slightly annoying when there's a queue of them behind you, making you push harder than you want to up the many steep hills on the route. One particularly useful camper van came along when my chain snapped in the middle of nowhere. Being a cycling novice at this point, I had all the tools apart from a chain link extractor and spare chain link. A mistake I will never make again! It was day three of the trip. We were only seven miles into the new day and my chain kept jumping. I looked down and to my horror, I could see that one of the links on the chain was sticking out slightly; a few pedals later, snap, the chain was no more. We were in the middle of nowhere; a little stone bridge offered a place to wait and flag down a passerby. It didn't take long to flag down a camper van and amazingly, they had a chain link extractor result! Then we realised they had no chain link, so it was useless; my heart dropped; what are we going to do? Will our trip now be brought to an end? We frantically googled bike repair places, with no luck, getting more and more worried that this may bring our trip to an end. How would we do the remaining miles if my bike couldn't be fixed? My mind started jumping to worse-case conclusions, as it always does. The next town along was Poolewe, so the camper van couple, who were going that way, welcomed me and my Bike and I got in, hopeful of finding someone who could help while my dad cycled the ten miles solo. I was very jealous to be missing out on miles but more worried about the remainder of the trip. We got there and there was nothing but a post office. My heart dropped; I didn't know what we were going to do. Then I saw a cyclist coming along, so I flagged them down, hoping they were local and would know someone or even have the tools we needed. As a result, they knew of a tiny bike repair shop in Aultbea…it sounded promising, so back in the camper van I got a few more miles down the road and amazingly, the "The Bike Shack' in Aultbea existed and the bike repair was a success! It was an old container in the middle of nowhere run by a man who repairs and sells old bikes. Imagine that life, living in the highlands, working on bikes all day. It looked so peaceful there and it sounded and looked ideal; if I could repair bikes, it would be a dream job, but I don't think he has any business competition to worry about with me! Let's hope for his business that there are many more idiots like me who cycle the NC500 without the correct tools!

I had no intrusive thoughts the whole eight days I spent riding my bike around the Scottish Highlands, none at all and this was at a time when I was struggling a lot back at home. Nature cured me for a while. Being outdoors where the only mission is getting to the next place on the map, pushing up hills, free-wheeling down, dodging the sheep, moving to the side for camper vans, speeding up when it rained and slowing down to soak up the sun and take in the mountains. My mind didn't have time to think of anything else other than what was in front of it, so I was able to slow down and take in my surroundings. My mind seemed to slow down, too.

My mind cleared; it was as if the fresh air that I inhaled took the toxins from my brain as I exhaled. I don't have the words to describe the beauty of the countryside I was riding through; you will have to go there for yourself to understand. I saw the sun setting behind the mountains in front of a loch; I saw ginger highland cattle with massive curling horns lying in the sun by the side of winding lanes; I saw thin, flowing rivers cutting down the sides of mountains and tall pine trees that scattered the landscape in every direction with their deep green bold presence, as if we were in Canada or New Zealand, or what I would imagine it looks like there. On our bikes, we were tiny against the trees, mountains, lochs and sea we rode through, little dots that wouldn't be seen from a plane. A journey not seen by others but felt so deeply by us.

We met numerous people along the way, some kind, some funny, some friendly and some not so friendly, all new people that won't be forgotten. It reminded me that all the interactions we have with others leave an imprint on life. Just being in the right place at the right time can lead to new friendships, memories and laughs. We met a man while we were sheltering from the fifty-mph wind who told us he'd driven past us in his camper van three times over the past few days. He said, "Have you heard of Audax?" I thought he was on about a town in Devon or something, but he soon explained that it was the long-distance cycling association. "You ought to look it up." It was this conversation with the man in the multi-coloured anorak that meant I discovered Audax when I got home, googling the strange word and finding a whole new world of cycling that I had no clue existed; more about this later. We met a group of women at a cafe who were in awe when we told them we had cycled up the Bealach Na Bar climb (a six km climb up the third-highest road in Scotland). We had a laugh at two local Scottish men who'd had a few too many and were singing in a pub and we got chatting to a B&B owner on the last night of the trip, who introduced us to her puppy, Teddy, a long-haired chihuahua that I slightly fell in love with and would have slipped in my pannier if I could have done. We met two men on the first day of the ride who were also cycling the route; on the fifth day, we bumped into one of them again, Dan. He was solo and he explained that his mate had also had a bike malfunction, but his was not fixable, his gear shifter had broken so he'd had to hitch a lift back to Inverness and go home, Dan was continuing the journey alone, no accommodation booked, he was taking it a day at a time, sleeping out in the open. A friendship was formed and he has since been over for a hilly ride in the Peak District with me and Kyle. That's the beauty of cycling: once you're in it, it's a community; it's like a secret you don't know about until you become a cyclist. You have a common ground that makes friendships form so quickly. It's nice to have people who will actually put up with the bike talk because I don't know if it's just me, but I find myself talking about cycling A LOT.

One thing for sure is that when I'm with my dad, the laughs are never far away; he's a character, to say the least! Equipped with his panniers stocked with enough food to feed an army and enough clothes to build a tent out of if we needed it, there were constant jokes flying about what he would pull out of his pannier next. Dan was in shock at the amount of stuff we had; I think my dad had brought an off-the-bike outfit for each night, a wash bag double the size of mine, two large packets of nuts that he never opened, about ten packets of cuppa soups, tins of soup (no wonder he was slow up the climbs), enough Freddos to open up a Cadbury shop, cake slices, packets of crisps and he was in every corner shop eyeing up the Scottish pies and pastries! But good on him, I say. We needed all the fuel we could get to help us carry all the stuff we packed with us and I was grateful that he had fresh clothes so he didn't stink out wherever we were eating! At one point on a little road that goes through Drumbeg, which can only be described as little in regards to its width, in terms of its hills, it's far from that, my front wheel lifted off the floor and I almost fell off the climb was that steep and the weight of my panniers was so heavy. As we reached the top of one of the climbs on this road, an old, abandoned-looking white house came into view. We heard indie music in the distance, which appeared to be coming from the house; as we got closer and sweatier, we saw a figure in the front garden, dancing to the music, giving us a cheer as we went past with a massive grin on his face, you see the most random things when out riding. That's one of the things I love: you head out on a ride, route planned and you can do the same route hundred times, but every time you do it, it'll be different.

As I sit here at my dining room table, the highlands of Scotland feel like a million miles away. But the trees, the cattle, the winding lanes and sandy beaches, the locals sitting in the pubs, the castle ruins towering over tiny villages and the small food stores filled with cycling snacks will all still be there, new people discovering its beauty every day. I feel so lucky that I have the memories and images that I can switch back to in my mind whenever I want. I hope I will have the images of what I saw strongly in my mind for years to come. That way, I can always go back; I can always feel a tiny bit of calm just by remembering.

Little mental health tip: Believe in yourself; you are capable of more than you think; it's better to try and learn from the experience than to not try at all.

When the Low Times Hit

I still go through phases of lowness and no matter how much riding, dancing on top of hills or yipping back down I do, it won't shift. Don't get me wrong; I still head out on rides; no mood is going to stop me from spinning my legs (or, as I like to call them, cod loins). But some days when I'm really feeling the weight of lowness, I don't even want to ride. I just want to stay at home, away from everyone. I don't let myself do that because I know going out will make me feel better and if it doesn't, at least it's a distraction for a few hours. I try not to get annoyed about it because I know that'll only make it worse, but it does annoy me. No matter what I do, no matter how much positive self-talk I run over in my head, no matter how many of the little mental health tips I preach, I feel Rubbish with a capital R. I'll say things to myself like, "Come on you've only got one life you've got to enjoy it" and my mind will say "I don't care about my life". It's as if I'm fighting with myself, so sometimes it's better to let the lowness win. I'm in one of these moods now and while I was cycling to work this morning, negativity was taking over; I didn't have the motivation to do my hair, telling myself I look ugly anyway, so there's no point. Pedalling along slower than usual on the cycle path, under the bridge by the river, over the hundreds of twigs, reluctant for the day to start but desperate for it to be over. I got a puncture yesterday and had to walk home, but that didn't dampen my mood, yet today, my mood is damp for no apparent reason. I don't understand my mind; does anyone understand theirs? I find it quite easy to pretend I'm okay when I'm around others; pretending can help; it forces me to be okay for glimmers of time, but as soon as I get home, I'm back to being down again. Other times, I don't have the energy to pretend and I'm quiet; I don't want people to notice, but they probably do; smiles are forced and my eyes don't shine. I hate that I can go from being so happy one day to feeling like I don't care about anything the next. When I'm in one of these moods, I feel heavy, and I don't want to be around anyone. It's like there's something pulling down on my chest, a bit like a heartbreak, but there's no reason for my heart to be broken. I can lose time just staring into nothing, the complete opposite of my usual hundred mph head that always has to be busy, always planning, worrying and going. It's like I've used up so much energy I have none left, a bit like bonking on a bike ride, but instead of my legs feeling empty, it's my soul that feels it.

Sometimes, the low mood wins and I'll make up an excuse to cancel plans and just be alone for a bit, not really speaking, just getting on with the day, waiting for the mood to lift because I know it will. Then I feel incredibly guilty for cancelling on a friend. I never tell them that it's because I'm feeling low; I'm a book full of excuses ready to go; sorry to any friends reading this; I love you, really! I don't even feel like seeing my family and if I do, I'm no fun to be around. It's as if I've had my share of happiness, so now I have to deal with lowness. The lows do make me appreciate the happy times more, but there's always a worry inside me: will the low time return? When I'm feeling happy, it sometimes feels too good to be true. There's a part inside of me that thinks I don't deserve to be happy and I don't know why. But luckily, there's a bigger part of me that tells that negative brain where to go and embraces the happy moments. I think that's why I get so hyper at times, especially when out on the bike. I'm just so grateful to be feeling good that it runs away with me. I don't drink, but if I told you I'd had one, you wouldn't have any trouble believing me when you catch me in a hyper moment! I just think to myself, you only have one life, so live it to the full and when I feel good and there are no thoughts in my head saying that my life doesn't matter or I shouldn't be here, I want to make the most of those happy moments and boy do I – so bring on top of the hill dancing, singing random songs as I ride, joking with whoever I'm riding with, hysterical laughter and yipes as I freewheel downhill because when I'm feeling good, I make the most of it and most of the time the bike can bring the good mood back.

Depth

There's so much deep inside.
Trillions of connections
Shaped by the world
A world so big.

There's so much deep inside.
Too much to explain.
Hidden cries
Behind eyes.

There's so much deep inside.
Thoughts never-ending
Worries
Deep and impending.

There's so much deep inside.
Hidden from the outside.

Things I Say to Myself When I'm Feeling Low

- Low times always pass and you'll feel happy again soon
- This is just a horrible feeling; it can't harm you
- You've gone through low times before and you can get through them again
- Put on some funny videos/ look back at happy memories
- Every day might not be a good one, but there's always something good in every day; find the good thing and hold onto it
- Never give up
- You have one life; make the most of every day.

Little mental health tip: Remember that thoughts are just thoughts. Thoughts are not facts. So, when negative ones enter your mind, tell them to do one, ignore them and throw them in the bin. They might keep passing through your mind like unwanted clouds, but you don't have to listen to them; they're just thoughts. Soon, happy thoughts will be back again.

The Thoughts – The Daytime Nightmares

I've always been a worrier. But the thoughts I experienced when in my state of unrest were like nothing I had ever experienced before. Horrible, horrible thoughts. Thoughts that made me feel like I had done something wrong. They filled me with so much fear and guilt that I couldn't focus on anything else. I truly thought that I was what my head was telling me...I was going to get struck off the nursing register because something bad was going to happen and it would be my fault. I had put people's lives at risk at work because of not being a good nurse. I had made a mistake at work and now someone might be in harm. These thoughts couldn't be ignored. They were on repeat and I had no off button. The more they came, the more I got wrapped up in them, the more elaborate and twisted they became. The more trouble I imagined myself getting into, the more of a bad person I believed myself to be.

The thoughts invaded my mind and took away who I was. I couldn't have a normal conversation with my husband without asking for reassurance that I wasn't a bad person and that I wasn't going to prison. I couldn't do the food shop, fill up petrol or paint the garden fence without a constant flow of intrusive thoughts pulsing through my mind.

When I was feeling strong and like I had some control over my head, it was helpful to think that all my thoughts had come from me. No one put them there. No one told me to worry. I did it all by myself. I had control over those thoughts. I could switch the thought from "a baby might drown in the swimming pool" to "the babies are going to love today's swimming lesson." (once I left mental health nursing, I taught swimming for a few months, something I've always loved, but the thoughts crept in there too; really, I needed to allow myself to rest completely, something I've always struggled to do). I may not have had a choice about the thoughts that crept in, but I did have a choice about how I reacted to them. I did have control over how I responded. I could put new thoughts in to replace the horrid ones.

Other times, when no matter what I did, the thoughts wouldn't go and I couldn't believe my replacement thoughts, it was more helpful to think that the thoughts were part of an illness that I had no choice over whatsoever. I had to learn to let them be there, not try to change them and acknowledge that they're very real, but they're not true.

Why my mind works the way it does is something I have become frustrated by a lot; why do I have to overthink? Why can't I just stop worrying? Why can't I be laid back? But I've come to accept that it's just the way it works. I worry and that's that. I don't want to start worrying about why I worry…that's too much worrying, even for me!

I'm beyond relieved that I don't have those intrusive thoughts anymore. And I can't put into words how grateful I am that I discovered cycling within all the chaos. When you're outside on a ride and you're cold and wet, your mind switches to survival; keeping warm, getting fuel and going in the right direction, you have no choice but to switch off from the other thoughts that are not serving any helpful purpose. This natural way of thinking helped me put things into perspective; my mind thought I was in danger, I was overstressed and these intrusive thoughts were a way of my mind trying to warn me and protect me, making me seek reassurance from everyone around me, but I didn't need protecting, there was no real danger. I felt like a weirdo, I felt alone, I felt like no one understood and I was scared to tell people about what my mind was thinking whilst at the same time wanting to tell everyone to get reassurance that what I thought wasn't true. I remember being on a dog walk, ringing my Gran and trying to hold tears back as I spoke to her about normal day-to-day things, cleaning, arranging to go for a coffee, asking how she was, but inside, none of what I was talking about mattered, because I was a failure, a bad person, I didn't deserve to have the family that I have. I knew I needed help. The doctors put me on Sertraline, but it made me feel out of it (I know this medication works for lots of people and I encourage anyone reading this to take medical advice); I didn't stay on it long enough to feel its effects. I had some counselling, which was helpful; talking to someone with whom I wasn't emotionally connected made me feel less guilty and less of a burden, but I was also scared to say too much; I didn't like the thought of people worrying about me. It was eventually mentioned to me by a doctor that I could be struggling with a form of Obsessive-Compulsive Disorder. I thought, no way, I don't have any compulsions, I don't have OCD, they don't know what they're talking about. However, they explained that there are different types of OCD and not all OCD involves worrying about cleaning, as the common stereotype goes. I knew this from my mental health nursing background, but I must admit I didn't have lots of knowledge about OCD. I was directed to OCD UK. I started to read a bit about it and things sounded familiar. I realised that maybe I did have compulsions; I was seeking reassurance constantly from those around me, googling cases of nurses being struck off the register to reassure myself that I hadn't done what they had and the intrusive thoughts were definitely there. I thought, great, here's another to add to the list: blooming heck, eating disorder, OCD, anxiety, depression. Am I actually okay? Then I realised that no matter what name you give each different part, they're all connected, they're all my mind, we created the diagnosis, but they don't stand alone. I needed to work on my whole self; I needed to get through this acute phase of mental torment and then work on my long-term mental health. So, I started going to an online OCD support group and it was the first time I felt less alone, hearing other people talk about the worries that devoured their day. I listened to the worries of the other people and thought to myself how absurd their worries sounded; there was nothing for them to worry about, really, it was all made up in their mind and as I explained my worries to everyone else in the group, I realised they would be thinking the same about me, my worries to other people were nothing to worry about, but to me, they were debilitating. From here, bike ride by bike ride, support session by support session, I started to get my mental health back on track.

The thoughts didn't disappear quickly; it was a gradual process, going from constant thoughts every waking minute to eventually being able to ignore them and then finally their disappearance. Where I am now is that I don't have intrusive thoughts anymore, but I am still a worrier; the worst-case scenarios always plan out in my head, but hey, at least I'm always prepared!

T here without reason
H appening inside
O ur deepness
U nderneath the mask
G rounded without evidence
H eavy when dark
T ricks of the brain
S wirling inside

It seems strange to imagine that there are two parts of you, but in my head, I have my 'me thoughts' (which, to be frank, can be very weird) as well as another set of thoughts which are more intrusive, more aggressive and more demanding, these are what I call the eating disorder thoughts or anxiety thoughts. When I was in the depths of my eating disorder, or intrusive thoughts phase, as I like to call it, it was hard to recognise the eating disorder/intrusive thoughts from my own; they didn't feel separate from me; they felt like part of me. It felt like those around me were the crazy ones; they were telling me that if I ate the piece of cake, it wouldn't make me 'fat' or 'unhealthy', whilst I would be sat there adamantly believing that I would instantly see fat on my stomach from one bite of it. Thankfully, I no longer believe this: cake is way too yummy to deny myself anymore and I enjoyed a piece of homemade cake and custard last night without a second thought; in fact, I'll be having another piece tonight!

The more I tried to recognise these negative thoughts, the more I started to notice how different they were from my regular thoughts, so I started labelling them as ED/intrusive thoughts. For example, when I see someone walking towards me whilst out in the middle of nowhere on a dog walk and my mind tells me they're going to attack me, I rationalise and tell myself, 'That is an anxiety thought and there is no evidence that is true.' So far, no one has attacked me and I also haven't been turning around and walking the other way like I used to!

Little mental health tip: Don't let fear stop you from trying something new; if you don't like it, you don't have to do it again, but you'll never know if you don't try.

Audax

Audax is a long-distance cycling association and they have become one of my favourite types of bike rides. After first hearing about it in Scotland from the man in the multi-coloured anorak and immediately googling it when I came home, Audax soon became a ride to aim for. They're not a race; there's no prize for finishing, although you do get a fully stamped brevet card (you collect stamps on your brevet card as you ride at control points to prove you've done the ride) and that's very satisfying! There's a cut-off time limit, but it's not fast, so it's inclusive for all abilities and they're pretty cheap to enter, usually around £5–£10 and you can usually guarantee a good bit of cake at the start and end, what's not to love?

My first proper 'long ride' was when I decided to cycle home to Derby from our caravan on the Llyn Peninsula in Wales. It was one hundred sixty miles and I did it in August 2021, a few months after starting cycling. I hadn't been cycling long and no real training went into it, but when I get an idea in my head, I have to see it through and I think my fitness was helped by having been a regular gym goer and jogger before starting cycling. It was a time when I needed an aim; I needed so desperately something to challenge me because I was spending my days feeling like a complete and utter failure for leaving my job. I needed to feel a bit of pain to prove that I still existed, to get rid of the numbness that had started to come over me. I needed to prove that I wasn't a quitter, that I could do hard things and that although I had left my job, I wasn't a failure. I said to Kyle, "I think I'm going to ride home from the caravan. Can we take my bike when we go there next week?" Kyle was as supportive as ever; he looked a little shocked but never doubted that I could do it; my dad, on the other hand, said, "Don't be so silly; it's way too far!" But that just added fuel to my desire to do it. So, at five a.m., on a rather misty August morning, before the sun had risen, off I set, me and my Carrera about to do our longest ride. The extent of my kit was: lights, trainers, gym leggings, a water-proof running jacket, a pump, an inner tube shoved down the back of my jacket and a running belt strapped around my middle with my phone and some snacks squished in. I hadn't yet discovered the comfort of cleats or padded cycling shorts. But I had discovered my favourite pre-ride fuel: a big bowl of porridge with peanut butter in, soooo yummy! I think I'd eat porridge for every meal if I could, I just love it. Recently, I tried some at a café with warmed apple and cinnamon lining the bottom of the bowl and that's becoming a new favourite. Every morning, I cook up a pan of the delicious stuff on the hob (if I'm in a rush, I begrudgingly resort to the microwave, I'll happily admit that I'm a porridge snob!) but on ride days, it always seems to taste better. With my porridge gobbled down, off I went with a wave from Kyle. I rode bumpily over the caravan field and turned left out onto the road, where I was alone. I'd been feeling alone, separate from the world for a long time, but as I pedalled along the lane, I welcomed being alone. It was bike time; my mind set on proving I wasn't a failure, my heart beating faster at the excitement of doing what I love all day and my eyes in awe of the sunrise ahead of me. I absolutely loved it, riding through the Snowdonia National Park, the only person on the road, with silence and an aim. Fifty miles in and I was at Bala, met by Kyle, who supplied me with some more snacks and a bucket load of encouragement. One hundred miles down and just sixty to go, a cafe lunch stop with Kyle gave me a little more encouragement, not that I needed it; Kyle said he hadn't seen me look so happy in months. Ten miles further along, my dad met me for the last fifty miles, equipped with his paper map and panniers full of snacks; he said he would take over the navigation from there. I trusted his skills, quickly regretting this, as four wrong turns later, we were back where we started. He then left his sunglasses on a wall, which we had to ride back to collect, but he did share his snacks with me, so I was happy about that. We eventually got to Hatton, the smell of the coffee factory a reminder that we were nearly back and a sign that rain was coming; two minutes later, the heaviest rain you can imagine pelted us. My dad wasn't happy about this, exclaiming, "I'm sorry, but you can't say this is enjoyable", but I was enjoying it; it was warm and I'd ridden my longest ride, a few miles more and I'd have done it! Mum welcomed us in; it was eight p.m., I'd done one hundred sixty miles and a passion for long-distance cycling was born; for the first time in months, I felt like I'd achieved something; I felt slightly less of a failure; I felt excited to plan the next bike challenge. A love for a post-ride curry was also born this day; we ordered a takeaway and ever since, curry has been my go-to post-ride meal – a Chicken Bhuna or Rogan Josh is my choice, with a Peshawari naan.

I did my first Audax on 24/04/2022, a one hundred sixty-five km ride which, in the eyes of Audax folk, is a walk in the park, but it was the only local one I could find and with it all being new to me, I wanted to start off small and build up, despite having done my one hundred sixty miles (two hundred fifty-seven km) ride the year before, my mind still doubted my abilities. I loved the little 'brevet card' you get given at the start, which you collect stamps or receipts in along the route to prove you've done it; perfect for making sure you keep the snacks coming in over the long day, as getting off the bike is a good time to get some food in, especially if you've not yet mastered eating on the bike. Occasionally, you have to answer questions such as what a sign says or the height limit on a bridge you cycle under; I'm not as much of a fan of these as I usually forget to bring a pen or cycle past the answer!

I have to say (and I'm sure the Audax crew won't mind) I've probably brought the average age of Audax down a few years and like all cycling, it seems to be very male-dominated. But I love the challenge of the long rides and the fact that they're not a race means it's less daunting and more accessible for everyone.

In May 2022, I did a four hundred km/two hundred fifty-mile Audax from Poynton to Holyhead and back (it's called the Llanfairpwllgwyngyllgogerychwyrndrobwll llantysiliogogogoch 400 – try saying it out loud! The ride is on every year so you can give it a go if you fancy it); it was my longest ride to date. The night before the ride, I told myself I wasn't going to do it, convinced something would go wrong or that I wasn't strong enough, but the morning came and I found myself getting in my Lycra at five a.m. ready for the two-hour drive to the start. At nine a.m. in the morning, I was off with a group of other crazy people who rode four hundred km for fun; my fear was about riding in the dark. I'd never done that on my own before and my mind was convincing me that I was going to get abducted or get lost or get a puncture and freeze. But Kyle, being the supportive husband that he is, was never too far away in his van, which filled me with the confidence to keep going, knowing that worst case, I could call him, but very determined that I wouldn't need to and could do it alone, I didn't want to have to ask for help. The halfway point at Holyhead is marked by a cafe, beans on toast were devoured, my brevet was stamped and I was ready for the next two hundred km. I met two men there who asked if I wanted to tag along with them; this was such a relief. I wasn't going to have to ride in the dark on my own if I could stick with them to the end! They were cycling faster than I would have done on my own, but the fear of being left alone in the dark pushed me to pedal harder; mindset on not being left alone, push push push is what I did. One of the men was in the police. Good job I wasn't having intrusive thoughts any more, or I would have cycled in the other direction! We stopped for fish and chips on the route back and Kyle met us there, joining in on the food, of course and, as usual, smiling in encouragement, telling me how proud he was and making me on the inside question how I deserve someone as good as him. Darkness came and we kept on going; the final control point was a service station, receipts were collected and wedged in our brevets, emergency sweets were eaten to give a last-minute sugar boost and the final thirty miles were done, a fist pump and cheer between me and the two men marked the end of the ride.

It was one thirty a.m. and to my surprise, I'd ridden at a moving speed of seventeen mph during the ride; at the start, I'd told Kyle to expect me back at four a.m.! I found his van in the car park outside the church in Poynton where I'd started sixteen and a half hours earlier and knocked on the back door; a tired-looking Kyle poked his head out and Chester lifted his head up from his bed then plonked it back down again, I squeezed myself in and onto the airbed, got a bit of pasta down me and slept squished between Kyle, the dog and my bike, full of a sense of achievement, relief and feeling glad that I didn't back out of the ride like I'd wanted to last night.

I did this four hundred km ride again this year (2023). This time, Kyle joined on his bike rather than in his van. Whilst on our honeymoon in March 2022, I was reading a book about the history of cycling and it mentioned an Audax called Paris–Brest–Paris. It's one of the oldest bike races around and it only happens every four years. Having ridden the NC500 a few months before and feeling full of the cycling bug, I blurted out to Kyle, 'In a year and a half's time, I'm going to ride Paris–Brest–Paris, you never know, you might get into cycling and do it too.'

Kyle said, 'No way am I doing that, but I know you will if you put your mind to it.'

Kyle caught the cycling bug at the end of 2021; I knew it would get him at some point! So, then Paris–Brest–Paris as a couple became our aim and Kyle found himself riding Audax's.

It was through joining a cycling club, Derby Mercury, that I learnt more about Paris–Brest–Paris, a ride that originated in 1891 with two hundred and seven cyclists from France (with women not being allowed to ride). Fast forward to now and where there are around six thousand riders who take part each year, unfortunately, there's still a tiny proportion of women compared to men. Only seven per cent of the riders were women in 2023. So, come on, ladies, if you like long-distance, get those bikes out riding towards PBP, the next one happens in 2027. It's a twelve hundred km Audax, which happens every four years and to qualify, you have to do a two hundred km, three hundred km, four hundred km and six hundred km qualifying ride, hence why Kyle also did the four hundred km Audax with me the second time around. Hearing my new cycling club mates tell tales of their PBP adventures made me both excited and nervous; there was so much to think about from the logistics of getting there to what kit to take, to when and where to sleep. It was over a year until the event was going to happen, but already conversations about it were flowing and one thing was for sure, I'd gone from reading about PBP whilst relaxing on the beach on my honeymoon to committing to riding it. When I first read about it, my initial thought was that I wanted to ride it, but I never believed I would be able to do it. Self-doubt always halts my self-belief.

Little mental health tip: Don't forget to look up; there's beauty in the sky above you that goes by unnoticed.

The Sky

I felt a moment of calmness one evening in the midst of intrusive thoughts. I was working as a swimming teacher after leaving my mental health nurse role and the thoughts had crept their way in there, too. All week, I had been worrying about getting sued by a parent at swim teaching, which, thankfully, I can see now was an utter waste of thinking space; the thoughts all stemmed around me getting in trouble. I was driving home from swimming teaching and while I was waiting in traffic, I looked up and was mesmerised by the pure blue sky. It had a dusting of almost transparent white streaks of cloud spanning from left to right. It was 8.10 p.m. I got out of the pool at 8 p.m. and slipped a towel-dress on to drive home in, spurred on by the thought of a stir-fry dinner Kyle was cooking at home on an evening where my world felt rushed and my mind felt full, just looking up and noticing the beautiful, clear, crisp sky, brought me to the reality that life is here and it's wonderful and I'm wasting it with all these worries. The sky lifted my mood with its brightness and made me see for a second that life isn't so bad; I can find a sense of calm and lightness by simply looking up. I gave myself a little mental shake. Amy, come on, look at this beauty in front of you; there really is nothing you need to be worrying about right now.

The sky is ever-changing; we don't always get the beautiful sky that I saw that night, but the blue is always waiting behind all the chaos of our weather. So, when it comes, embrace it, go out and enjoy it, watch it and feel safe in the calmness it brings. You can guess when the blue sky might come by looking at the forecast, but the best times are when it comes by surprise. Unplanned moments of happiness that come without the burden of expectation that is when true happiness is felt. It's like when it's been raining on a ride and the sun comes out for the last ten miles to dry you out and remind you that you love cycling. On that evening, on my drive home, it had been a rainy day, both literally in the weather of the world and in my mind, so walking out of work to that sky was a welcomed surprise that cleared the stormy weather of my mind for my drive home.

Little mental health tip: Practice being kinder to yourself. Every morning, say one nice thing about yourself when you look in the mirror. It might be really hard to do, but it gets easier the more you do it; you have so much beauty inside and out.

The Mornings

Waking up and feeling sweat on my chest was not a rare occurrence during the worst times. Luckily, these days, sweat is only on my chest when I've peddled my way up a leg burner (aka a climb), usually in the Peak District or on an Audax. In the morning, I can usually tell how the day is going to be by how I feel when I wake up. On the anxious days, I wake up with a feeling in my chest that is hard to describe. It's not a pain and it's not a flutter; it's just a feeling of heaviness or discomfort that won't budge. I feel edgy like I need to get up and move about and I don't want to sit still, but at the same time, the thought of getting out of bed and facing the day is exhausting.

In my time off between jobs, the anxiety meant I couldn't lie in and catch up on the sleep I'd lost to nightmares and worrying; as soon as I woke up, I felt the need to get up. My mind would be alert and planning out my day before I even woke up. Staying in the comfy sheets just wasn't an option; if it wasn't the physical feelings of anxiety that made me get up, it was the guilt that my husband was going to work and I wasn't that made me get up and try to be as productive as possible.

Although waking up in the depths of illness wasn't always the most fun experience, once up, I found the early mornings out walking my dog quite calming. Pavements peppered with early morning dog walkers like myself and roads empty apart from a few cars infrequently passing by, leaving my phone at home so I could walk without distraction. You can hear birds singing, the sky is dull as the sun is only just rising and the air feels cool on skin that hasn't woken up properly yet. There's a misty feeling in the air that wraps you up; you become part of the air flowing around you, feeling half asleep, the outdoors waking you up. This is something I still do every day now; it gives me a chance to think without distraction and just be. Of course, I now cycle to work each day too, but I can't say this is as calming of an experience; I need another walk by the time I get to work to re-set; let's just say traffic and people in a rush to get to work doesn't make for a happy cycling experience!

Little mental health tip: Before you go to bed, turn off your phone, the TV and any other screens and spend a few moments digesting the day. Ask yourself: What went well today? What would I change about today? What am I proud of myself for? What will I do better tomorrow?

The Nighttime Nightmares

Sleep should be a rest from the madness of the day. But nightmares can destroy the peacefulness. Annoyingly, daytime worries can find a route to seep into dreams and create a real-life reenactment of your fears in high-definition pictures for your eyes only. It's annoying how the mind doesn't seem to rest in the times when it needs it the most.

You lie down in bed, hoping to get some rest, plumping up the pillow, wrapping the duvet around your body, feeling snuggled up. Warm and cosy, but you don't feel calm. Your mind whirs round and round; the same thoughts that have been occupying you all day seem determined to continue through the night. The more you want them to stop, the stronger they get. You toss and turn, desperate for the thoughts to stop, to have just a minute where your mind is quiet. You eventually get to sleep, only to be woken by vivid nightmares that leave you feeling even more uneasy than you already did.

Waking up in a panic after a nightmare is a horrible feeling. I hate the moments afterwards in the middle of the night. It feels like the whole world is sleeping; there are no external sounds, no light, no traffic noise or bird calls. All you can feel is the internal beating of your heart and all you can hear is your husband's deep breathing next to you. For a little while afterwards, your pulse beats strong and you feel dazzled by the brightness of the images in your mind. The nightmare slowly fades as you realise that you're in bed. You lie there, slowly accepting that the nightmare wasn't real, but not certain that it has gone away; any moment, the images could flash back into your mind. You feel worried about closing your eyes again, just in case the images come flooding back. The true feeling of relief is in the morning when it's light and the nightmares can't return until the next night.

When I was at my worst, at the most, I got a maximum of a few hours of sleep a night. The nightmares made me feel like I hadn't slept at all. I woke up feeling more tired than when I went to bed. But I woke up, I got out of bed and I remained determined not to let this thing in my mind beat me. Luckily, I'm now in a place where sleepless nights are a lot less common. I get the occasional spouts of not being able to get comfy, feeling like the night is lasting forever and I'm not getting any sleep, but on the whole, I sleep like a baby, no nightmares to be seen, things always get better.

Even when feeling overtired and low, I would still look forward to the Sunday rides with my dad. Cycling gave me something to look forward to. The idea of doing a few more miles this Sunday compared to last Sunday or more elevation was something that gave me a buzz. After a ride, I think it was the endorphins that made me feel the happiness I'd been missing; it was like the lowness lifted the further I pedalled. And there was something about being out with my dad that made my sense of responsibility lessen, which is what I needed at the time. I was worn out from the responsibility I felt as a nurse, so going out cycling with my dad, who did the route planning and bike fixing, was bliss. All I needed to do was turn up on time and follow my dad along, pedalling, enjoying the views and not being needed for anything other than to keep my dad company.

These days, I go out solo a lot more and plan my own route, feeling braver on the bike, venturing further and hillier and always on the hunt for the next challenge; I have the desire to see what my body is capable of and push myself further. Although I must say, I feel a lot better when riding with others in terms of any mechanicals going on! I'm trying to learn more about bike mechanics, especially following a puncture incident where, like a damsel in distress, I had to call Kyle to come out and help me after failing to get the tyre back onto the wheel, tubeless on my list to do, I don't seem to have much luck with punctures! I also absolutely love planning routes now, although Kyle isn't as keen because I usually chuck as many hills in as possible; the more hills, the more opportunity to dance on top of them (more about that later).

Little mental health tip: Take comfort in the fact that we are only human; it's okay to make a mistake or get something wrong. Living life is complicated, but you're living it and there's so much to enjoy when you let the worries go and be kinder to yourself.

The Birds

I can remember a day in the middle of spring when stuff had really hit the pan and I was still working as a nurse, trying to convince myself and everyone around me that I was okay, even though I'd spent all night worrying about something I didn't need to and itching to get on my laptop and check the notes I'd written the day before, to double check I had done them right. I woke up and heard the birds singing outside; I immediately knew it would be a better day than yesterday. I sat in front of the mirror in my bedroom; I closed my eyes for a second and listened.

When you find a moment of stillness in the midst of the busyness, sit in that moment for as long as you can.

I imagined that I was a bird; if I was a bird, then all my worries would be insignificant. I sat as a bird for a few minutes. Then I had to snap back to the reality of being a human and 'get on with it', as I like to say.

Birds have always stayed as birds, living their flying lives, building nests, reproducing and singing their songs, much like all the other animals. Humans, on the other hand, haven't stayed as we are, living to standards that don't ever end; there is always more to achieve, new standards to meet and pressure everywhere. I don't know if it's just me, but my brain isn't very good at not seeing endpoints to success; once I've done one thing, I crave the next. It's something I'm working on, trying to be better at doing less and not feeling bad about it – I say as I sit here typing whilst in the back of my mind feeling a little lazy for sitting down rather than being on the bike, ED mind creeping in and quickly being shot away by my rational brain – you starting to see how silly my mind is?

We've created, innovated, adapted, progressed; we're not just here to reproduce but to succeed, earn money, impress others, meet social standards, get followers on social media, follow the rules; we've even created robots to do the things we don't want to do. In a weird way, knowing that we created the stressful situations and turned the world into the way it is now kind of reduces the stress of the stressful situations – we made this all up anyway, so let's make up less stress; there's no real right way to do life, we created 'the right way' why can't we uncreate it. Things like which career path to take, what age to have children, what clothes size you are and how many likes you got on your Instagram post are all just another measure of comparison that is totally irrelevant...be happy in life; that's what matters. The birds that fly past you each day aren't worrying about the next day; they're not worrying about whether the bird next to them has better feathers, is fitter than them or lays better quality eggs; they're just birds, just being. Maybe we should try to just be humans, just live; that is enough.

I suppose cycling has helped me to go back to being a basic human again because when you're out on the bike, the only thing that matters is getting to your destination safely. You're right in the middle of nature, you're part of nature and because you're on a bike, you're moving at a pace (unless you're an elite cyclist) that you can truly take nature in; you can see every stone on the road, every leaf on the tree, you notice the animals in the fields, the clouds in the sky and you realise how small you are compared to the world around you and how small all your worries are, more importantly, how irrelevant they are; whatever thoughts are in my head, the world still turns.

Little mental health tip: When everything feels overwhelming and like you have a million things to do, write a list and do one thing off the list at a time. Tick each task off as you complete them and remind yourself that it's okay not to get everything done all at once.

Cycling Is Becoming Part of Me

I guess in life, we get the most satisfaction from the things we actually want to do, the things that we have a burning desire inside to achieve. Instead of feeling pressured to reach goals, we reach for them out of our own passion and determination. The enjoyment and feeling of completeness when I'm cycling comes from inside me and no one is making me feel judged or that I should or shouldn't do something. When I think about it, it's rare to find other areas of life that someone else doesn't influence. I couldn't imagine my life without cycling now; it brings me so much happiness I can't fully describe it. If I could spend all day every day cycling, I would. I can't say every moment of every ride is enjoyable; if the wind is in my face and I'm battling against it, or it's freezing, for example, a time in Glencoe, in Scotland, whilst riding LEJOG, Kyle got a puncture and I was so cold I had to star jump on the side of the road to stay warm and it took about forty minutes to fix because our hands were so cold we couldn't unscrew the valve cap to get the tyre off. But on the whole, the bike is my happy place; there's the enjoyment of completing a challenge, soaking in the sun on summer rides, the views, the cafe stops, freewheeling downhills, sounds of nature and the social element which I never expected.

The more I've started cycling, the more that little element of competitive nature has been brought out, mainly pushing myself to go that little bit faster or tackle a few more hills. But it doesn't feel like something I have to do; it's something I want to do and enjoy; as long as it stays that way, I'm winning.

Little mental health tip: All the minutes that we spend beating ourselves up or comparing our lives to others are minutes that could have been spent being happier.

Conversations on the Bike

Most of the time, my head is full, continually full of non-stop chatter: putting myself down, planning my day, planning my week, getting excited about future bike plans, questioning what I am doing with my life, getting frustrated at myself, talking myself down, snapping away the negative thoughts and boosting myself up, worrying about insignificant things that feel significant, good mood days creating happier thoughts, low mood days dampening them, it's a whirlwind up there. My mind naturally jumps to worries and what-if scenarios. I've definitely gotten much better recently at reminding myself that thoughts are not facts, but there are times when, no matter what I do, the worries overwhelm me. When the anxiety is high, I usually get pre-ride worries; I'll convince myself that I'm going to get mechanical that I won't be able to fix or I'll get run over by a car, but once I'm out on the bike, as soon as my bum hits the saddle and my legs start moving, the worries go. A positive mindset seems to take over when my feet clip into the pedals and whatever comes my way, I'll handle it. This positive and determined part of my mind helps me get through the long rides when my body feels tired. I find it so much easier to talk myself positively through long rides and keep my spirits up when I'm riding compared to any other area of my life. I must admit I'm not so positive when I'm trying to change a tyre and it's taking me forever, but I don't think many of us feel positive about punctures!

My head keeps me peddling when the weather is bad or when that last ten miles of a hundred-mile ride feels a little bit too far. I use positive self-talk to prevent me from giving up, "You can do this, Amy." I picture the end feeling and I remind myself of harder things I've gone through before. When I'm out cycling on my own, I can sort of measure how I'm feeling mentally by what thoughts I'm having; as I've said, the majority of the time, my rides are worry-free, but there are rides that aren't so sweet; if I'm putting myself down a lot or worrying, 'you're not going fast enough', 'you're probably going to get a puncture', 'what's that sound on your bike? Is it going to break?' then it's a sign I'm probably a bit stressed or anxious and maybe I need to see what my balance in life is at the moment. When the stressed mind is around, I think about how I can add in a bit more rest and downtime for the next week. When things are going well, I'm not worrying, I'm not pressuring myself to go a certain speed, I don't find it hard to choose what to eat at the cafe stop and I'm just enjoying being out.

Alongside the chatter in my head, riding in a group with others who share the same passion is a community that is full of conversations. There's something about cycling along next to someone that opens up conversations you wouldn't expect. It's like the bike is a safe space to speak about whatever comes to mind. You're not sitting staring across a table at someone, so the conversation flows easily and you just feel able to share – well, I do anyway! I've had some of my most open conversations whilst out on the bike; things I wouldn't normally speak about seem to spew out and people have shared things with me; it's nice to speak out in the open; the sound of the wheels and wind in your ears meaning only the person riding next to you can hear what you're saying, unplanned therapy on bikes between friends.

I love that you get people of all ages, from different backgrounds all riding together, no hierarchy or social status involved, no one cares what job you do or what your house is like and no one knows what you look like in your day-to-day life, I saw a club member, Gordon who's a teacher when not on the bike, in a suit once and I barely recognised him! When you're cycling with others, you're cyclists, that's it. Yesterday, I went out on a bike ride with a couple from the club, Nige and Jan. They're the same age as my parents and they're basically mine and Kyle's bike parents; Nige helps me out with learning about bike maintenance and tells us off if we go too fast on a social ride or for filming him too much...he loves the camera really! We did a fifty-mile ride and met up with an eighty-two-year-old club member, Jim Hopper, who still cycles on a daily basis, three generations cycling together and the conversation never stopped flowing. It was amazing to hear all of Jim's cycling stories, including almost handing his notice in at work when they told him he couldn't have time off for a bike event. He laughed when telling me that he once fell off his bike on the way to work and when they gave him the day off, he decided to go out cycling all afternoon. He also told tails of Paris–Brest–Paris, which he has done eight times, that's thirty-two years' worth of twelve hundred km rides.

Not all rides involve lots of conversation, the fast club rides where your heart is beating out your chest, sweat forming under your armpits and down the centre of your back, you clinging on the back trying not to get dropped, breathing is the only thing your mouth can do. Conversation isn't an option as you just about manage to breathe. The ride ends with red faces and a feeling of relief, knowing that you have worked hard and it'll pay off in your future rides. The post-ride chatter comes and once everyone can breathe again, laughs are always had after the final sprint to the end. Some rides, if I'm not in a good mood day, I don't talk a lot; I just listen to what everyone else is saying. Taking in the conversations around me, just listening to the chatter of others makes me feel less alone and distracts me from whatever negative thoughts are going on in my mind; it's enough to slowly lift my mood and by the end of the ride, you probably can't shut me up. That's the great thing about cycling: you can ride whatever way suits you: group, solo, fast, slow, chatty, silent, in Lycra, in jeans, cleats or trainers. As long as you're out on the bike, you enjoy it and it's what you want to do that's all that matters.

Disconnecting

Everywhere we go, we're followed.
We're followed and we're followers.
The world can see us, but can we really see it?

We display a version we want to be,
A version others want us to see.
No time to meet you in real life
My mind is too occupied with my device
No time to sit down and talk
It's easier to text and walk.

Disconnect?

Something that seems so easy to do,
But it is only possible for a very small few,
Your true self comes when you find what's right
For me, that's riding my bike.

*Little mental health tip: You can get through more than
you think; your mind is strong, you never give up and you
can get through hard times.*

Not Wanting to Live

The hardest thing to think and write about are the times when I've felt like I don't want to live anymore. I've battled with whether to include the depth of this chapter, partly still feeling shameful about it and worried about sharing, the other part of me knowing that it's not just me that has felt like this and that the more we talk about it, hopefully the more people who are struggling will be able to reach out for help. In the worst times, the intrusive thoughts got so bad I didn't feel like I could bear to withstand them. I felt like I couldn't keep going. When the intrusive thoughts faded, I was left with a sense of failure at leaving my job and a lowness hit; I felt worthless, like a burden on my family, like I'd never find another job, like I was pointless. I felt as low as when I was in sixth form. I thought that it was all behind me, but it was back. I've always had low phases, but this one was the worst I've experienced. I've never tried to end my life, but I've thought about it and I've planned it. There was a time during lockdown when tablets had to be hidden and Kyle used to call me a few times a day to check I was okay. I can remember one of my lowest days. I was having a shower and I just felt awful; it was a Saturday, Kyle was working and I felt like everything was pointless. I had everything I needed, I was loved, I didn't need to worry about finding another job because my teaching swimming and Kyle's work was just about enough to pay the bills, I had a house, water, food, a comfy bed, friends, clothes, but I wasn't happy, I felt like a complete failure, like I wasn't doing enough and that I shouldn't feel like I do, I felt full of guilt for feeling down, I knew that I had so much, yet it didn't change the way I felt. I urged every part of me to feel better. I wished I could feel happier, but I couldn't; no wishing would get the lowness away. I felt like my happiness would never come back and I felt like a burden on my family, especially on Kyle. Tears streamed down my face and I wished I wasn't here anymore; I didn't want to deal with what I was feeling any longer; I thought maybe today I just won't be any more; I don't have to deal with my head anymore and no one else will have to deal with me. Then Chester walked into the bathroom. He looked up at me crying and I looked back at him. 'He needs me to feed him and he needs a walk; I've got to be here.'

Something inside always stopped me from following the plan I made. I always knew deep down that life is worth living and I have to withstand the low and anxious times because happier times always come again. I think of my family, of my happy place in Wales (more about that soon). I go for a ride and I remind myself that things are not always this bad. Since leaving the mental health field, having a less pressured work life and finding cycling, my mind is more able to rest. But I do still go through phases of feeling like life isn't worth living and thoughts of not wanting to be here are something I've become used to. But I can deal with the 'life is pointless' thoughts much better now as I know they will pass and mentally I'm in a much better place. And I say, yes, life may be pointless, all the more reason to have as much fun as possible; it is better to live a happy, pointless life than a sad one.

I first got thoughts about not wanting to live in sixth form. I felt different to everyone else. Now, I've come to realise we're all different to everyone else and that's a good thing. If we were the same, the world would be boring. But I felt different in a way where I felt like I couldn't join in conversations properly; I had no motivation to. I felt so stressed about getting A*s in my exams; maybe the pressure I put on myself wore my mind out. I was also dealing with my younger sister going through anorexia, so that could have played a part. But really, I don't know why I started to feel this way and I don't like to trouble myself questioning it. That's the thing about mental health: there doesn't need to be a reason why; maybe there isn't a reason, maybe it's just the way my brain thinks.

When I go through low moments, I get times where I can't get the 'what is the point in all of this?' feeling away. My mind spirals down into a negative path of 'we're all going to die anyway', 'I'm not doing enough', 'earning enough' the list goes on. I have a feeling that takes over my whole body, a feeling that makes me feel low, pointless and misty. I can wake up in the morning with the feeling, or it can come over me all of a sudden, like a rainstorm on a summer day. No matter what I do, the feeling won't shake away; it stays there, firmly planted in my core, until another day. I have to accept that these days are the hard days. The feeling could be described as a sigh that flows from the roots of my hair to the nails on my toes, taking over me and bringing an air of lowness. It's as if the fire that keeps me motivated has burnt out and it won't come back on without a bit of time for new fuel to be gathered. So, I have to wait it out, sit with it and accept that this is the way I feel right now, but it will pass. On these days, sometimes a ride doesn't even help; my spirits will lift while I'm out on the bike and I'll yipeeee down some hills and push harder up them, burning my pent-up energy and annoyance at feeling how I do, but when I get home the bike buzz soon wears off and I'm craving the next ride to get my boost. When this happens, I know that I need to give myself time to let the low mood pass; I can't block out feelings with a ride; I have to face them.

When the happier days come and the fire is re-lit, I'm able to think in a more positive way; if I'm going to die anyway, then I might as well make the most of my life, live it to its fullest and stop sweating about the small stuff. I have one life and I want to live it.

My love for cycling has helped me in unbelievable amounts with the low days; it really is my medicine. I'm not sure if it's the endorphins from exercise, the adrenaline of free-wheeling down long hills, or the calmness found on the small lanes that I cycle on that helps, but it makes me feel alive and gives me a purpose again; it makes me feel free.

A note I made on my phone for the low days:

Today, all you need to do is:
 Hydrate and nourish your body with food that you enjoy
Wear comfy clothes
Say no to things you don't want to do
Talk to yourself the way you would talk to a friend
Take breaks
Spend some time outdoors
Talk to someone you love
Remind yourself that today is just one day.

Little mental health tip: Remember to take time for yourself. Life is busy, but it's okay to slow down and focus on the moment you're in because once the moment is gone, you never get it back.

Crash

It's December 2021; the NC500 ride with my dad was three months ago and it feels like much longer than that. Last week, I set out on a fifty mile or, as I like to say, milone bike ride. I woke up, got ready as I usually do and left the house at about ten a.m. It was a weekday and I was teaching swimming in the evening, so I had the day to ride my bike. I planned to be home by two p.m. and spend the afternoon walking the dog and doing a bit of cleaning before heading to the swimming pool. Little did I know what the ride had in store. Since I started cycling about a year ago, the only incident I've had on my bike is being blown into a sheep fence in Scotland and that didn't leave a mark, thankfully. But last week a mark was left. It was twelve thirty p.m. and I'd done forty miles, just ten miles until home. The ride had been a great one, just a solo spin, taking it steady and feeling grateful for the warmth that came from pushing up hills, as it was quite a cold day. I was wrapped up well: thick gloves and lots of layers, including a fleece; this was before my days of Lycra wearing and cleats. I stopped off just before a roundabout to double-check which way to go; I'd changed my route mid-ride. I'm not sure why, but I just fancied a change from my usual loop. I set off again, unaware of what the next few minutes were going to bring. As I was coming around the roundabout, I saw a car approaching to my left and soon realised that it wasn't going to stop. As I thought to myself, 'That car isn't going to stop', within what felt like a mili-second, I was hitting its windscreen and then the road. I saw a flash of the blue sky, heard a crunch, crack and skidding sounds and found myself lying on the tarmac road. Bike just out of reach, car tyres within inches of me. The instinct in me was to launch myself off the floor as quickly as possible because I didn't want the car to run over my body; the immediate thought in my head was, "Move, or the car is going to go over your body, I don't want to die". I leapt up to get to the side of the road, or so I was told by the witness; it's all a bit of a blur. The next thing I knew, I had the driver's jacket around me and sat in his car; they took my phone and scrolled through my contacts to call Kyle and my mum. Kyle was working only three miles away at a building site and came skidding around the roundabout in his van, fear in his eyes and relief when he saw I was talking, although he said I looked like a deer in the headlights. A few moments later, my mum was on the scene; the next thing I knew, I was in her car being taken to A&E (the wait for an ambulance was too long). We decided that it was best for my mum to take me as Kyle gets quite stressed in these situations, so he went home to the dog and my mum kept him updated by phone. The drive to A&E felt like a lifetime. The first thing on my mind was letting down the children at swimming, worried about what the swim academy boss would think and then

I burst out, "Omg, my new bike, Mum, my bike, is ruined!"

My mum calmed me. "Amy, a bike is a thing, the most important thing here is that you're okay."

I was in such a daze I couldn't really think about it, but sadness filled within me, I loved that bike and it was only my second ride on it. Then I started thinking about the broken windscreen. "Omg, I've broken that man's car windscreen, I can't afford to pay for him to have a new one."

My mum looked at me strangely. "No, Amy, he ran into you, don't worry about that!"

"Mum, I don't need to go to A&E. I'll be fine."

Mum, with her fully functioning brain, "Amy, you've hit your head and you've been hit by a car; we are going to A&E."

Filled with adrenaline, I thought that I was okay. We pulled up at A&E and went up to the reception desk. I could just about walk, but it felt weird.

"What's your name and date of birth?" asked the young-looking and smiley receptionist.

"Amy Hudson, twenty-ninth March 1996," I just about forced out; suddenly, what had just happened seemed more real.

"Thank you and what's happened?" she asked in a calm tone.

"Well" – tears started to form in my eyes out of nowhere – "I've just been hit by a car."

The receptionist's eyes widened. "Just now? Right..." She looked a little panicked called out to a college. "Can we get this lady a wheelchair and take her through to red room, please?"

Before I knew it, I was being wheeled into another room, placed carefully on a bed and a neck brace was put on me, my head hurt, my back ached a little. I started to feel a pain in my legs but nothing was excruciating. An MRI scan was had a few hours later and I was sent home with a head trauma leaflet and a physio referral. After a sleepless night, waking up the next morning in a lot of pain, I realised that I wasn't as okay as I thought I was, my elbow the size of a tennis ball and a dull headache persisting, but, luckily, I was more okay than you'd think I would be if you saw the car; its windscreen completely smashed with an Amy-like body shape. So, I'm currently writing this as the concussion is wearing off...I probably shouldn't be writing at the moment; I should be resting, something I find incredibly hard to do. I'm feeling grateful that there are no broken bones, just soft tissue damage that will be fixed with physio and time; the whiplash isn't fun, but it could have been worse. I bought a new helmet only weeks ago and if it wasn't for having a good quality one, I dread to think what would have happened; the helmet cracked, but it prevented a worse injury to my head. The beautiful Ribble bike that I'd saved up all my swim teaching money for months was written off. I'm gutted about it, but like everyone has been telling me, bikes are material; you're not.

Some people have said to me if I wasn't wearing that helmet, I would be dead or severely brain damaged; if I had not landed how I had, it could have been so much worse. I've had suicidal thoughts, but after this, it's made me realise how much I do want to be here and I feel so lucky to still be alive. I can't run or cycle at the moment, but I can talk and I can walk. I'm meant to be cycling Lands End to John O Groats (LEJOG) in May, in five months' time and I'm still determined to do this. I will have to work hard with my physio and allow myself to rest, but I know I will do it.

We've fast-forwarded a bit. It's almost a year after that crash now and after eight months of physio, I was pretty much back to normal again; I got back on the bike after two months, despite being told I should wait longer, but my heart was being pulled towards the pedals and my eating disorder brain was trying to make a return, the lack of exercise making me find eating hard enough, I made the decision that short rides would be beneficial for my mental health and with close supervision and support from the physio, I was back loving riding again and building up the miles to ride LEJOG, more on that later. Unfortunately, I don't have the best track record with cars, as in January this year (2023), I was hit by a car again! Fortunately, it wasn't as bad as the first time, but again, the driver didn't see me; I was pulling up to a junction to turn right, just about to come to a stop and a car came from my left, they turned right onto the road I was on and instead of staying on their side of the road, they cut across and straight into me, another bonnet for me to roll over. Flashbacks of the first crash filled my mind and I found myself in a tearful panic attack in the middle of the road again, my bike just out of reach; a couple who were walking past ushered me to the pavement and rung Kyle, who came to the scene within minutes, I was less than a mile from home and on mile ninety-nine of a hundred-mile ride. I've had to have physio round two and there's been a big knock to the confidence, but I got back out on the bike again as soon as I could; I love it too much to let it stop me. This time, I was riding on my canyon, a beautiful blue and pink bike that I got through insurance, when I was hit by a car the first time around. Again, it's been written off and this time, I will admit I cried about the bike; I loved her. But the driver admitted fault, apologised numerous times and a new bike is here.

I still miss my first carbon road bike, my pink and blue Canyon; memories were engrained into the carbon frame, shattered by a simple mistake. It's strange how a connection can form with a bike; it's just an object, but you go through so much with it, it feels like so much more than a bike, it's sort of like a companion. You don't realise this until you start cycling. I actually used to find cyclists a hinderance on the road; little did I realise the unexpected beauty of bike riding, but now that I'm part of this secret happiness society, there's no looking back. After the crash, I was able to get a gravel bike and a road bike, a Canyon Endurace for the road and a Cannondale Topstone for gravel rides. I also used the gravel bike for long road rides, as her kingpin suspension means she's super comfy and, yes, I do call them her/she, they're like my babies! I actually give them names too, don't judge... The Cannondale was named LB for Little Beast and the

Canyon a more simple Canny. If you told me a few years ago that I'd think so much of bikes, I would have laughed and not believed you, but now they really are a massive part of my life. Fast forward to 2024, where I am now and I somehow have a bike sponsor, and it's blummin' Pinarello! My mind is literally still comprehending how this has happened. If you'd told me time last year, I'd have thought you were pulling my leg (or should I say my chain) because to me, having a bike sponsor is just a dream that I never thought was within my realm. Somehow, I now have two Pinarello bikes for the year and I can't blummin' believe it. When I was asked to be an ambassador, I thought someone was having me on. I refused to believe it was real until I got the bikes home. But it is real, as real as the carbon X7 Endurance bike currently sitting right next to me. I picked my new baby up a few weeks ago; a trip to London to collect her felt like a dream, especially as I whipped around Richmond Park, in awe of how smooth she rides and of seeing the deer as I rode along! I did nearly roll into what I've been informed was a Canadian goose in my excitement, but luckily no bikes or geese were harmed. I've decided to call her Pinny. I like to keep the names simple. I'm picking up my gravel bike next week, a Grevil for tackling a bit of off-road and I've already decided she'll be named Rella; this sounds a bit more gravel-esk, I feel! Never in a million years did I think starting social media channels would lead to this, but here we are and I'm trying to ignore all the thoughts in my head that tell me I don't deserve it. Kyle is over the moon as he's now the proud owner of both Canny and LB and has also been given a Pinarello for the year too. He also still has his steel bike, a Ribble which he uses for Audax's, so he now has four bikes and has lost the right to moan about taking photos for me! But it is only material; the memories live on in my mind.

Little mental health tip: Write a list of reasons to smile. When feeling low, reasons to smile can seem impossible, so make your list when you're in a good mood and look back at it when you're not feeling so good.

My reasons to smile today: the sun is out, I got the consistency of my porridge right at breakfast this morning, I have a loving family who are always there for me and a new book I ordered is meant to arrive today.

Useless

I feel so useless at times; I don't know what I want to be or what I want to do with my life. Ever since the crash and I've not been able to teach swimming, I've felt like a spare part, a cog that's not turning. I'm not contributing to life like I should be. The only thing I really know is that I love my husband, my family, my dog and cycling.

When I could finally cycle again after eight weeks, getting outdoors on my bike was the only thing that made me feel that life was worth living. When I came home from a ride, the lowness would prevail before I even had time for a shower…I've done my bike ride now; what next? I'm going back to swim teaching, but I'm becoming increasingly more impatient about what I want to do with the rest of my life. I want to find a new career path, but I haven't got a clue where to start.

This is when I started to feel useless in the forefront of my mind and where I realised that maybe I've always felt a little useless. The more I thought about it, the more I realised that maybe we all feel useless at times; maybe no one really knows what they are doing or what they really want to do; we're all just living life the best way that we can. I remind myself that I am lucky to be alive and push the useless thoughts away, ignore them and throw them in the bin. I'm not useless; I'm here, living life and I'm going to enjoy it.

Heavy

Life lies heavy
On heads that think too much
Life lies heavy
On hearts that give too much
Life lies heavy
On eyes that see too much
Life lies heavy
On ears that hear too much
Life lies heavy
On souls who give too much
Life is heavy.

Little mental health tip: Reach out to someone you love and tell them how much they mean to you. It will not only make them feel good, but it'll give you a little mood boost, too.

The Caravan

The place where I feel the calmest (apart from on the bike) is at the caravan; our place in the middle of nowhere in North Wales where you're lucky if you get a phone signal and when you step outside, you hear nothing but birds singing, cows mooing and the occasional training RAF jet flying over. At nighttime, there's no light pollution at all, so on a clear night, you can look up and be dazzled by endless stars. I love the feeling of stepping out onto the cold patio, shutting the door behind me and just looking up. It reminds me of how small I am and how much there is to be discovered, of how insignificant all my worries are and of how amazing the world is. Sometimes, when I'm feeling stressed, I remind myself of the stars at the caravan and that the stars are above my house at home, too; I just can't see them as clearly.

The caravan is on a small caravan site next to a farm. There are only six caravans and they overlook a beautiful view of rolling fields down towards the sea in the distance, where at nighttime, you can see the lighthouse flashing every few seconds. There are a few farms in view, cows and sheep dotted in the fields, the emptiness of the countryside bursting with nature, not people. The little lane that I take when doing a ten km jog (more frequently before starting cycling) can be seen from the front window of the caravan. When I get to that point, I look across to the caravan, usually out of breath and questioning why I'm doing it, then reminding myself to breathe and take in what's around me and stop pressuring myself to go faster, one step at a time, breathe in breath out; this isn't a race, the only person who cares how fast you go is you, so if pushing yourself to go faster isn't fun, try enjoy going slower.

I think the fact that it's always there and it's not changed is what I love about going to the Llyn Peninsula; I've been going to the caravan since I was a baby and my dad has been going since he was a child. Every time we go, it's always quiet; the sheep and cows are always in the fields, the trees are always green and the woods behind the caravans are there, albeit the trees are taller now than when I was young. But it's always there. No matter what happens in my life here at home, the caravan is always there and when we go there, it feels like nothing has changed; I could be back as a ten-year-old again, getting stuck up trees in the woods and going on adventures to make dens in the fields. My dad's told me numerous stories about him going there as a kid, one where he was chased by a goat and had to dive under a barbed wire fence (he still has a scar on his back to show off); he used to spend the whole six week summer holiday there, exploring, bird watching, going out on his bike all day, worrying my Gran when he didn't come home on time and looking forward to the food van that came to the site once a week to stock up their supplies. We would go at least twice a year when I was growing up, but no bike for me; I didn't enjoy cycling at that point. Walks in Snowdonia, colouring books and playing in the arcades in the local town as a child are all memories that I wish I could slip back into in real life at times; what I'd give to have the child responsibility-free on holiday feeling again. I do kind of become a bit like a child, full of giddiness when I'm out riding my bike; maybe that's why I love it so much; it brings out my inner child again because I'm discovering something new.

The calmness I feel when I'm at the caravan is hard to describe; it's as if all the heaviness from my body is temporarily lifted. It's like the relief you feel after expelling a big deep breath, except it lasts for the whole time I'm there. The caravan in Wales is my sanctuary. It's our own private retreat; no, it doesn't have a swimming pool, morning yoga classes or meditation sessions, but just being there is enough. Even when I was struggling the most, Wales was able to bring me a sense of calm. Whilst off work, when I no longer believed I was going to prison but was struggling with feeling low and anxious, I went to the caravan with my mum and dad for a few days. I felt so guilty for going. Kyle was at home working, but he encouraged me to, knowing that it was my happy place. It felt so nice to be there after the chaos of the last few months. I remember sitting in the little lounge, looking out over the unchanged view, the same view I've seen looking out at since I can remember and thinking to myself, "What an earth happened this last year?". COVID, breakdown, leaving my job, finding cycling, feeling lost, feeling like I don't want to be here, desperately grateful that I am here and now here I am, back at the place that's always here. I reflected that I needed to do what makes me happy. I spent some time wishing that I could just spend my life cycling or living in the caravan, but then I reminded myself that I have to work to enjoy these things and when I got home, I started applying for jobs and found myself in finance.

Everyone needs to find what their sanctuary is and use it. On my tough days, I imagine I'm in Wales and a tiny bit of me lifts.

Little mental health tip: Be kind to your body, nourish it, hydrate it, move it, speak kindly to it and say sorry for all the times you've criticised it.

My Sister's Comment

One day, I was at a coffee shop with my sister, chai latte on order, of course and she said to me, "I can't understand why anyone would want to end their life, why they would do that". I didn't really say anything because I didn't want to get into it. But in a strange way, it made me happy because if she can't understand it, then she hasn't felt it and I don't ever want her to feel it or understand it on that level because that will mean that she won't ever want to end her life. She seems to have an innocent view of life and a carefree spirit that I wish I had. She doesn't question the reasons why we are here or what the point of life is; she just lives it and I hope she and lots of other people can live their lives that way.

Little mental health tip: Be happy for the success of others; if someone else has achieved something amazing, that doesn't make you any less of a person. The world would be happier if we cheered each other on rather than put each other down.

Don't let the success of others make you feel less.

Weeds

I was digging weeds out the drive on a summer morning, the type that grows up through the cracks in the concrete and seems to multiply daily. After an hour, my back was aching and I was ready to give up. The roots were so deep and I knew that no matter how much weed killer I used, within weeks, they would be back. I persevered because I wanted the drive to look nice and I knew if I let a few little ones stick around, they'd annoy me every time I walked past and only grow bigger.

It's crazy how something so small that looks so fragile on the outside takes up so much strength and time to get rid of. They root themselves in and they won't leave without a fight; even when you think you've got rid of them, they come back. I suppose, in a way, humans are a bit like weeds (the pretty ones that look like flowers, of course); it's not always clear how strong we are until we're challenged; we all have hidden roots. Our strength comes from a place that you don't see unless you ask. Whatever mistake we think we've made, no matter how many times the thoughts in our heads cut us down, pull us apart and spray us with weedicide, we all have the power not to give up; our roots can regrow.

Little mental health tip: Always have something planned to look forward to so that when things get hard, you have a reason not to give up.

Feeling the Rain

I went for a run this morning on a cycle track that's only a few minutes from my house. Occasionally, I run, but cycling is my preferred sport, as you've probably gathered! As usual, while I was running, my mind slipped into thinking mode: what shall I make for tea tonight...I wonder what Kyle is doing at work...I need to let my boss know about the new kid at swimming...I should text my sister when I get back...I'm meeting Maria for a coffee on Saturday, which means I probably won't have time for a bike ride...I need to do the washing when I get home...the list could keep going. Then it started raining and I was brought back into the moment; the dampness of the rain forced me to focus on my environment. I started to notice what was around me rather than the thoughts and plans about the future – the trees with their autumn colours, the old man hobbling along with a walking stick who smiled and said good morning as I jogged past, the lady jogging with her earphones in looking like she was ready to give up, the fields surrounding the track and the new houses being built in the distance, the cockapoo chasing a springer spaniel who didn't want to be chased, the man all dressed in black cycling with big panniers on the back of his bike, all while the drizzle slowly soaked through my clothes.

I got home with my mind feeling fresh and my skin soaked, Chester in need of a bath. It made me reflect on how so often we are living through the eyes of the next moment, meaning that we miss the moment we are in. Or maybe we don't miss the moment we are in, but we don't fully live in it. I constantly plan what is happening next and when I eventually get to the moment I've been thinking about, I'm planning the next one. It's like we live life in fast-forward, but we don't have a rewind button. It's so hard to live in the moment and part of me feels like the 'live in the moment' trend is another pressure that's hard to fulfil; how do you stop thinking about the future or the past when there is so much to be done or so much that has been done. I don't think 'living in the moment' is easy or achievable all of the time, but I think you can have small pockets of it and maybe the more you focus on it, the easier it gets and, hopefully, the more enjoyable life will be. For me, being more aware of where I am and trying to slow down my mind is the start of a very long way to go. You don't have a receipt for the day; you can't return it and re-do it; one chance, spend it wisely.

Little mental health tip: Don't worry about your 'failures'. The majority of the world has no clue about them.

Embrace Being Insignificant

It's pretty hard to comprehend the amount of people in the world. The number of lives that you know nothing about. The amount of people that know absolutely nothing about you and probably never will do. Every day when you leave your house, you pass by people that you know nothing about, people you will never see again. It makes me feel so small when I stop to think about how big the world is. I take comfort in how insignificant I am. I like being insignificant because it means all the mistakes I make or things that don't go how I want don't really matter because the majority of the world will never know about them anyway. When I think about this, I feel reminded of how important it is to try and enjoy my life as much as possible and stop stressing about the little things. You don't need to leave a big imprint on the world; you don't need to have achieved anything amazing; living life in a way that makes you happy is enough. In my eyes, enjoyment of life is the biggest measure of success (okay, maybe I don't always believe this, but I try to). We're only human and all we can do is live life the best that we know how to. I was on a club ride just last week and as I was standing at the end with a few others, an old man walking past started chatting to us and he randomly said, "It's nice to be important, but it's more important to be nice. You all seem like nice people." And that's stuck with me because it's so true: just being nice to others makes life so much more enjoyable both for you and the person you're nice to.

We are all in different circumstances; for some people, enjoyment might be easier to find, but at least try to open your mind to the possibilities that could come your way. It's okay to feel upset about our insignificance and it's okay to feel happy about it. We are all different and that's what makes life so interesting.

Little mental health tip: No matter how hard the day ahead seems, remember that it's just one day; you've got through so many before, you can get through this one. Make your aim to find one good thing about today and tell yourself that this time next year, you'll be looking back, proud of all the hard days you've gotten through.

Facing the Day

This is a memory from June 2021, when I had just left my job as a nurse and was teaching swimming.

I stood on the landing at the top of the stairs at home, packing my swimming bag ready for work ten minutes before needing to leave the house. I felt overwhelmed with anxiety, a sense that something bad was going to happen. Thoughts flooded my mind that I would instruct the classes wrong and a child would get hurt. That a parent might hurt themselves when they are getting into the pool with their baby because I asked them to get in wrong. These worries really scared me.

I knelt down next to my bag, tears pouring down my face, trying to calm myself down. Breathing deep, pressing toilet roll into my eyes to stop the tears. Squeezing my temples with my hands. Repeating to myself, 'Everything will be okay. Come on, you can do this. I wiped my tears, got changed and took deep breaths all the way into the car. Radio on and trying to focus on the words. I wear a mask of happiness and calm when I get there. No one suspects that inside, I'm struggling, doubting my every instruction, overwhelmed with my mind. Teaching goes well as it usually does, parents happy, children smiling – well, most of them, not all babies are a fan of the water. But I come away with other worries, overthinking about the child who coughed after swallowing some water or the child who cried.

I don't know when I got to the point of fearing the worst in everything, of worrying about seemingly silly things.

But I make myself face my fears. It is painfully hard. I wish I could stay at home next to my swimming bag and that the ground would swallow me up. That I could drift back to bed, go deep under the cover and not come back out. I don't know when the thoughts are going to stop. But I have to face them. If I retreat into my bed, I might never come back out. So, I face the day; I face the day every day.

It actually makes me quite sad to think about that time; I'm so grateful to have gotten through those moments and carried on. I had counselling on a weekly basis and having that space to express my worries really helped me, as did escaping on my bike and coming home to a supportive husband. Looking back now, I know I didn't give myself a break after leaving my job as a nurse, I should've stopped everything. I should've had time off with no work at all, but I couldn't allow myself to do that because I already felt like too much of a failure.

Little mental health tip: At the end of the day, write down three things you are grateful for.

Connecting with Nature

I feel most at peace when outside on my bike in the middle of the countryside. I feel at home in nature and I guess that's because we are nature; what the trees exhale, we inhale, we're connected.

If you haven't been to the countryside for a while and are in a position to be able to, I urge you to spend some time there; I find it has so many benefits, both physically and mentally. It brings me a calmness that I can't describe well enough.

For some reason, I always feel like my worries are far away when I'm in the middle of nowhere. I can't describe in words how much it can change my mood, but it feels like the weight my mind has been carrying is cleared by the freshness of the outdoor air.

The other day, I went on a ride, but when I got up into the hills, it was so misty that I was scared that the cars wouldn't see me, especially when free-wheeling down the small, windy lanes. But I kept peddling and I focused on keeping safe (I had my lights on and was wearing bright colours); I kept telling myself that the further back down the hills I got, the less misty it would get. I never give up when on a bike ride and I will never give up on life because now I remind myself that the mist always clears.

Although I didn't get the views on the misty ride, I still felt a sense of calm, more so when the mist cleared. Just being outdoors, away from the busyness of modern life, is enough for me to keep going and not give up.

I feel so grateful for nature and I appreciate every second I spend in it.

Little mental health tip: You don't need permission to love or like yourself; you have the power to make it a reality. Start by speaking more kindly to yourself and let it build up from there. Whack out some Post-it notes, write down things you like about yourself and things you are proud of yourself for on them and stick them around the edge of your mirror.

Lands End to John O Groats

The trip details:

Day one – Lands End to St Neot – seventy-four miles

Day two – St Neot to Silverton – seventy-six miles

Day three – Silverton to Wookey Hole – sixty-nine miles

Day four – Wookey Hole to Little Dew Church – eighty miles

Day five – Little Dew Church to Wem – eighty-one miles

Day six – Wem to Wheeldon – seventy-nine miles

Day seven – Wheeldon to Oxenholme – sixty-five miles

Day eight – Oxenholme to Gretna Green – seventy-eight miles

Day nine – Gretna Green to Larkhall – seventy-nine miles

Day ten – Larkhall to Tyndrum – eighty-six miles

Day eleven – Tyndrum to Fort Augustus – eighty-two miles

Day twelve – Fort Augustus to Alness – sixty-eight miles

Day thirteen – Alness to Tongue – sixty-eight miles

Day fourteen – Tongue to John O Groats – sixty-nine miles

What a journey! If I could do it all over again, I would. May 2022, two weeks, just me and Kyle, cycling across the UK, discovering new places, getting drenched, soaking up the sun, dancing on top of hills and yipping back down, punctures at the worst possible times, cafes found at the best times, enjoying chai lattes, cursing headwinds and praising tailwinds, meeting new people, packing, unpacking, pushing, freewheeling.

I can't sum the trip up easily because so much was discovered and it felt like it lasted an eternity. We decided to make the trip over two weeks so that we didn't feel rushed; we wanted to take in every moment and enjoy it rather than pedal as fast as we could, more of a cycling holiday than a rush across the UK (although it is on my agenda to try and do it a little faster). On this trip, all my home worries faded, just like when they did on the NC500 with my dad. When you're on a cycling holiday, your focus is purely on the moment you're in and getting where you need to go. Your worries turn to survival, food (where's the next cafe? Hot chocs and chai lattes are a must), keeping warm, cooling down, hydration, not getting lost, preparing for all possibilities, motivating yourself and each other, not arguing when you get lost and learning to cope with each other's hanger. It was on this trip that I started to document my cycling on Instagram @Amy.cycling.adventures, thinking it would be a bit of fun but also with an aim to inspire others to join in with cycling and spread some mental health awareness, knowing how much it had helped me. Never in a million years did I expect it to grow to the level it has; I'm just Amy, but somehow, some people are interested in what I'm doing.

Spending two weeks on the bike makes you think about all the insignificant things that you waste time worrying about and about all the things you wish you spent more time doing. It makes you realise how big the world is and how much there is to discover; it makes you crave more. It challenges you; Kyle and I survived two weeks in each other's pockets and let's just say it wasn't all rosy; cycling through four hours of torrential rain, feeling cold and not being able to find anywhere for food wasn't a recipe for the best of moods. But we got through together, supporting each other along, apologising after shouting at each other or making a remark in the heat of the moment, laughing off the argument when we both cooled down. It creates new connections; we met so many people, a couple in the Lake District who had travelled here from America, their bikes had front and back panniers, they didn't have cleats and they were spending three months cycling around the UK. A man and his wife on the top of Cross of Greet in the Forest of Bowland, they'd cycled up one side and had just realised if they carried on their route downwards, they'd be cycling back up the long drag again later; his wife didn't look too pleased, but off they went freewheeling down in the hope of finding a cafe for lunch – us cyclists do like our food! We met a man by Lake

Windermere who knew Geraint Thomas (very jealous) and again took a photo of us, little memories snapped; every picture we have comes with a little story and we can't help but smile as we recall. Whilst navigating through Glasgow and getting lost trying to re-find a cycle path that was shut, we met a helpful cyclist who was on his way to work. He told us that he worked for UCI and spoke enthusiastically about the cycling world championships due to be held in Glasgow next year. He helped to direct us back onto the cycle path and we were very thankful as I think we were a few pedals away from an argument; Kyle and I are not fans of getting lost! From there, we rode to Luss for a cafe lunch with a hot chocolate each before embracing the four hours of rain that accompanied us to Tyndrum. But we were again met with kindness; the hotel staff ushering us in, letting us leave our bikes locked up in a side room at the hotel and advising us how to get the heating up in our room so our kit would dry out. That night, we ate at a fish and chip shop, but it wasn't just any old fish and chip shop, there was a few things on the menu you wouldn't expect and homemade cakes filled the counter. Kyle, being a man of tradition, devoured sausage, chips and beans whilst I set my sights on a chick pea curry with banana bread for pudding. Bellies full, we headed back to the hotel, where the stench of our cycling kit drying on the radiators in our room almost knocked us out when we opened the bedroom door. But we were both so tired, we had no trouble falling asleep, until we were woken numerous times in the night but a faulty fire alarm!

Not everyone we met was nice; Kyle was called a 'nob head' for refusing to give a drunk man a 'backi' on his bike, which I found hilarious. We also had our fair share of the drivers who, for no apparent reason, gave us a beep or middle finger. But by avoiding as many main roads as possible, the quiet country lanes were blissful and it truly was a dream trip.

It's on this trip that the top of the hill dance and the phrase 'cod loins', which is what Kyle and I call our legs when cycling, were developed. On day two, we had the biggest climb of the trip, one that I had been really excited about, Dartmoor. It was a hilly day: seventy-five miles/ one hundred twenty km with seventy-two hundred ft/twenty-two hundred meters of climbing. The climb was tackled after a little breakfast in Tavistock, granola and yoghurt for me; Kyle opted for a full English, which slipped down the gullet a treat! Snacks in our jersey pockets and off we went, Kyle not looking forward to the climb, me very excited about it. We rode up the country lane, which cut through fields of sheep; I shouted, "Hello, sheepie", as I usually do, my breath getting deeper the higher we went. For most people, I imagine this climb wouldn't be a lot, or maybe it would; I know there are much bigger climbs, especially abroad and I have my eye on a few, but at this moment, this climb was big for us and on reaching the top I decided to do a little dance, I don't know why, I just had the urge to do a little jig, what can be described as the same dance the donkey in the film Nanny McPhee does…from then on I always dance on the top of hills when I'm on a ride because it feels good, yes I look silly, but I don't care, we only have one life and in hundred years' time no one will remember me so I'm not going to worry about looking silly anymore! Now, the phrase 'cod loins', I have no explanation for at all. I think it was Kyle who said it first and we just kept saying it, so no, we're not referring to a fish and chip shop; we mean our legs. "Oh me, cod loins" is a common phrase when the two of us are out riding. I love the little random things that come out of bike rides; when I'm cycling and I get giddy or tired, sometimes a mixture of both, new phrases sprout out! Knick-knacked is another of my favourites, or "I'm ding dang didlio", which basically means I'm tired.

My dad was meant to be joining us for the LEJOG adventure, but he pulled his back a couple of weeks before as he wasn't feeling up to doing the full route, which was over a thousand miles' long (we opted not to do the traditional route, wanting to avoid main roads and instead riding on as many quiet lanes as we could). Not wanting to miss out completely, Dad joined us in Fort William on day 11 of our trip. His arrival brought with it the usual dash of energy that my dad sprinkles wherever he goes. We were so glad to see him as we had just cycled through Glencoe in torrential ice rain; I'd been so cold that I hadn't been able to change gear for the past five miles, my fingers losing all strength. Somehow Dad managed to bring the sun with him and the rest of the day was glorious. We rode along with views of Ben Nevis, singing random songs and feeling grateful for the weather change. We finished the day riding along a cycle path which led us to Loch Ness and Fort Augustus, such a beautiful little place that I wish we'd had more time to explore.

Although Dad was only joining for four days, he had more stuff loaded onto his bike than Kyle and mine put together; no wonder he'd pulled his back! Two big panniers filled to the brim, his Trangia made an appearance, along with a ground sheet for us to sit on at lunchtimes and enough snacks to last a month. It was lovely to have him along with us for the last four days, he's the one who took me out cycling in the Peak District when I was at my lowest, managing to make me laugh when I had forgotten what feeling happy felt like. I'm forever grateful, because without those weekend rides in the Peaks, I don't know how I would have kept going. Although his faffing around, particularly in the mornings, was slightly irritating, the laughter he brought outweighed the annoyance of us starting later than planned each morning. His snack choices always made us laugh; one day, he came out of a shop with a large pack of marshmallows and after we had a curry for tea one night, we all went in search of puddings at a co-op. He came out with cake, a tin of custard and a mini bottle of wine as well as more tins of soup to heat up on the Trangia the next day. He devoured the cake and custard in bed, after scouting out a spoon and tin opener in the communal kitchen where we were staying. We all shared a room that night as it was the only option; Dad was demoted to the sofa bed!

When we got to John O' Groats, we were filled with pride at reaching the finish, but this was tinged with sadness that the adventure had come to an end. We free-wheeled down to the LEJOG sign, yipeeeeeing all the way, but both of us looked at each other with a hint of, "I don't want to reach the sign, because then this is over." in our eyes. If I could, I would have ridden back to Lands End again; I just wanted to keep riding. I felt the happiest I'd felt in a long time on this adventure and I didn't want the feeling to end. My lovely mum drove all the way to John O' Groats and was there waiting for us when we arrived. We all stayed at a B&B together, the same one Dad and I stayed in when cycling the North Coast 500 the year before, so I was very excited to see Teddy the chihuahua again! The next day, Mum and Dad got the train home (my dad used to work for the railway so they get free train travel all over the UK!), whilst we made the long drive home. When we got home, we immediately booked to cycle the NC500 (round two for me!). We couldn't face the thought of not having another trip to look forward to and since this was the place where my passion really grew, I wanted Kyle to experience it. I booked the annual leave off work straight away, wrote it on our wall calendar in the kitchen and crossed the days off as they passed, images of the Highlands filling my mind and sleepless nights of excitement formed as it got closer.

Little mental health tip: Set yourself something to aim for and work towards it; having an aim is great for motivation and helps on the down days. Of course, I recommend entering an Audax...but whatever floats your boat or, should I say, spins your wheels!

NC500 Round Two

The trip details:

Day one – Inverness to Lochcarron – seventy-one miles

Day two – Loccaron to Gairloch Sands – eighty-three miles

Day three – Gairloch Sands to Achmelvich – ninety-seven miles

Day four – Achmelvich to Tongue – eighty-nine miles

Day five – Tongue to Altnaharrah – seventy-six miles

Day six – Altnaharrah to Inverness – one hundred five miles

So, four months later, in September 2022, we set on the NC500. I was full of excitement, knowing how amazing the first time around with my dad was. We started off by getting the sleeper train from Crewe to Inverness. To keep the cost down, we opted for seats rather than beds; let's just say we won't be doing that again; one man chose to lie on the floor to have a chance of getting some sleep; it was that uncomfortable. The woman next to me had no issues sleeping and her snoring kept me up all night despite the earbuds I was wearing. But I was so excited to get back on the highland roads that a little lack of sleep wouldn't dampen my spirits. Once we dropped off some clean clothes and toiletries at the hotel, we'd pre-booked for a week's time when we returned to Inverness, off we pedalled. Six days, five hundred miles and even more smiles. We were so lucky with the weather, only being caught in the rain twice over the whole week and for a maximum of two hours. During one rain shower, I saw another cyclist ahead, equipped with two large panniers and a bright yellow raincoat. She was hard to miss, a dot in the distance that became an aim to catch up with; as I got closer to her, the writing on the back of her raincoat became clearer: "The rain always passes". This gave me a little boost and sure enough, the rain did pass just in time for us to stop for some lunch. Whenever I'm on a rainy ride at home, I remind myself of the stranger whose raincoat gave me a little smile and positivity on that horribly rainy morning in Scotland.

We stayed mainly in youth hostels and a few B&Bs. The first night, we stayed in Lochcarron, choosing to tackle Bealach Na Ba (the biggest climb on the route) at the beginning rather than the end of the day. We stayed in a little B&B the first night, run by an elderly lady, Moyra, who walked slowly, with shaky hands and a strong Scottish accent. It felt like we were guests in her house rather than a B&B, a house that hadn't seen a decorator for a while, patterned wallpaper, a green-coloured bathtub, ornaments filled endless cabinets and thin glass windows that looked out over Loch views, a scene that's not changed for centuries. It felt cosy and safe like we were staying at a long-lost grandparents' house. Moyra took our breakfast order before we went to bed and at eight a.m., our stomachs lined with a cooked breakfast, we set off on day two and towards the big climb.

The biggest climb of the route, Bealach Na Ba, wasn't as hard as the first time around, likely because I didn't overpack this time! As I pedalled up, a year on, I reflected on how much had changed in the last three hundred sixty-five days; my mental health was the best it had been in a long time, I was in a job that I could switch off from, I could go to sleep without worries controlling my mind, I felt pure happiness without a drop of doubt, I had cleats and wore Lycra and I felt hopeful for the future. The view around me was breathtaking and I could fully take it in without any worry about returning home once the ride was over because I was finally feeling happy again and more myself than I'd ever felt in my life. I realised that if cycling could help me this much, it must have been what I was destined to do. Don't get me wrong; I'm not happy all the time. I don't think that's possible, but happy times are here a lot more and for that, I was grateful as I pushed up and on, sweat starting to form on my forehead that soon evaporated as we reached the cool top. A few camper vans passed, a lot less than on my previous trip. The end of COVID caused holidaymakers to go elsewhere and cheers of encouragement were called as they went past. I took a few moments as I climbed up to stop and look back, the breathtaking view behind me of water cutting down through the green and other mountains in the distance. We reached the top, passing a group of deer on the final corner, a final motivator to push to the end. As we rolled along the flat top of Baelach Na Ba, dark clouds started to form, the top of the climb less picturesque than the climb itself, so we quickly took a picture, wanting to dodge the rain and down we yippeeed. The peak of this climb is a little disappointing, but the views on the way up make up for it, so if you ever ride it, take time to soak in the views and look back. Kyle is much braver than me on the downhills, but I always stay close enough to keep him in sight; halfway down, I saw him skid and fling into the grass on the right-hand side of the road. I peddled faster, head going crazy; he's hurt himself, we'll have to call an ambulance, the bike might be ruined, we might have to cut the trip short…but as I got closer to him, I saw him launching himself off his back, cleat wading through the long grass onto the road and on seeing he and the bike were okay I burst into laughter and so did he, I just wish I could have got it on camera! He took a corner too wide and luckily, the thick grass gave him a soft landing, so only his dignity was damaged as he lay on his back with his legs in the air. We took the rest of the descent a little slower, staying next to each other and freewheeling to the Applecross Inn. We were too early for the pub, but with just a ten-minute wait for the outdoor shack that served hot chocolate and flapjack to open, we waited, rain jackets on as the clouds overflowed and sipped hot drinks under a gazebo, bracing ourselves for the next few hours of rain as we looked across to the Isle of Sky.

The whole trip was like a dream: one of the most beautiful moments was seeing a clear sunset and sunrise at Achmelvich Youth Hostel, which has the most beautiful little beach and a fish and chip shop, which is closed on a Wednesday, the night we were there! Kyle was not best pleased, but his spirits soon lifted when curry and ice cream were on the youth hostel menu, it was like home away from home. Tagging along with a group of cyclists from Holland for a few hours was fun; they weren't fans of the climbs! We met some motor bikers who were also doing the NC500 loop; they spoke to us in awe, saying they couldn't imagine cycling the route; they were finding it tiring enough on their petrol machines; they took a picture of us with our bakery snacks, we didn't share them, sorry! We met a cyclist at Tongue Youth Hostel who was on a year-long bike-packing trip; he was planning on heading south through Britain and into Europe. He told me about the Transcontinental Race, something I hadn't heard about but looked up there and then. It's a self-supported bike race that goes across Europe, one of the hardest ones around, something that seems way out of my league at the moment, but there is a little part of me that sees it as an aim for the future. I've since read Emily Chapell's book "Where There's a Will" and have been to see her talk; she's an inspirational woman who won the Transcontinental in 2016. She started off as a bike courier in London and went on to become who she is now: an amazing ultra cyclist. I've since learnt about Jenny Graham, another inspirational female endurance cyclist;

she's from Scotland and is the fastest woman to have cycled around the world unsupported; her book "Coffee First, then the World" is a real page turner that takes you through the depths of her astonishing accomplishment and inspires you to take on challenges. Sometimes, when I'm riding along, I imagine I'm Emily Chapel or Jenny Graham, wishing their strength and ability into my legs, then I start to feel tired and realise I'm still me, although I'm sure they get tired too!

Day four of the trip brought a re-visit to the Drumbeg road, the little hilly lane which was home to a steep climb I'd walked up the year before with my dad due to my front wheel leaving the concrete. This year, I was determined to make it up the climb; as we headed towards it, I reflected on how much my cycling had come on over the year. I ride every weekend now and I'm not scared to go out solo. I'd ridden a four hundred km Audax, I'd discovered cycling shorts, carbon bikes (not that you need a carbon bike to have a good ride or be a cyclist! Although, their light weight does make the hills easier) and clip-in shoes (cleats), I now knew what a QOM was (a queen of the mountain, which is the fastest person on a strava segment) and I had a sat-nav on my bike, tracking my mileage and my speed, but these things didn't make me any more of a cyclist compared to when I just rode a few times a month in my gym clothes with my dad. Anyone who rides however they want to or in whatever way they can is a cyclist. My carbon bike and cleats didn't make the second

NC500 trip more enjoyable; I enjoyed both of them just the same; yes, maybe I was more comfortable the second time around, but my mind was mesmerised and full of happiness on both trips. This year, with more cycling strength inside me, the hills on this road were a lot easier and no walking was had; I think I partly have learned to pack light, too, with fewer clothes and more snacks in my bike bags and no panniers to be seen, instead a seat post and handlebar bag with only the essentials were brought along on the trip.

The memories from this trip could go on forever: watching the deer from our bedroom window at Althaharrah B&B on our second to last day, where we were cooked a homemade meal in the host front room (we chose to route back through the centre of the highlands rather than ride on the busy main road on the east coast). The couple that runs this B&B are lovely; they actually come from Burton on Trent but made a move to a more simple life in Scotland; they offered to wake us up in the night if the Northern Lights were out, of course, we said yes, but no knock on the door came, the lights weren't out that night, but seeing deer from our bedroom as the sunset made up for it. This memory of our final night is tinged with a bit of sadness as we went to bed that night, our trip almost coming to an end. The final day back to Inverness didn't start off in the best of spirits. We had a block headwind and with both of us feeling a little tired, we had a few tiffs; at one point, Kyle slammed his hand down on his handlebars and shouted, he was fed up with the wind and hadn't eaten a big enough breakfast too, the hanger was setting in. But on reaching the lovely village of Dornoch, which we detoured to as I remembered it being a good cafe spot from the last trip, I had one of the best hot chocolates I've ever tasted at Cocoa Mountain and Kyle filled his pockets with sweets from a local sweet shop, after all, we were on holiday! Our spirits lifted and we spent the final hours on the bike in high moods; we even had a second cafe stop at a farm shop cafe; it wasn't planned, but we couldn't resist it and a jacket potato with tuna went down a treat. We loved the end of our ride, pedalling closer to Inverness and deciding we would finish the trip with a curry at the same place I finished the ride at a year before with my dad. We checked into our hotel and to my relief, the stuff we dropped off six days ago was still there; never have I appreciated some clean clothes and my wash bag so much. Showers were had and we lay down on the big king-size bed, feeling like we were in a palace compared to the bunk beds at the youth hostel we had been sleeping on a few nights ago. Slipping into sleep with the highland winds still encapsulated in our hair and images of cattle, thin roads cutting through mountains and the rough Atlantic Ocean within my eyes.

Every moment of that trip has been savoured and firmly planted in my memory bank. Another place that I can return to in my mind whenever I want to, back to the mountains, long stretching roads and peace and quiet.

Little mental health tip: Stop, relax your shoulders, soften your brow, relax your tongue inside your mouth, scrunch up your toes and then let them go. Take three big, deep breaths; everything is okay.

The Little Stresses of Life

When I came back from Scotland, I reflected on how easily stressed I get when I'm at home. I feel like there is so much more stress in life than what's needed. Sometimes, when I'm anxious, I get so worked up it feels like there's something in me that needs to come out; it's like I could explode, a panic attack brimming but not coming. I want to tense up everything from my fists to my toes; I want to shout and cry; nothing makes me feel better; whatever is in me won't come out until it wants to, so I have to wait, try to rationalise and remind myself it's just a feeling. I sometimes imagine a simpler life, moving to the middle of nowhere where there is less busyness and more calm. Less traffic, less noise, less rushing around. I watched a documentary about a man who lives in the middle of nowhere on his own in the highlands of Scotland the other week ('The Man Who Lived as a Hermit for Forty Years'). He's taken remote living to the extreme and he seems genuinely happy. I'm too connected to my family, friends, routine and warmth to ever take a leap that big; I mean, wild camping for a night, I can cope with, but I need my home comforts. His stressors are about survival in the rawest sense: warmth, food sources and weather. He's not comparing himself to anyone else or chasing the next fashion trend. It seems like a lot of us have forgotten how privileged we are to live life, not needing to worry about warmth or obtaining food. Instead, we're worrying about how we shape up compared to other people, how much we weigh, how tanned we are, the brand of our shoes or the smell of our perfume. I hold my hands up; I'm a culprit of it like so many of us are; it's the way we live, but I try to be more grateful for what I have and remind myself that one day, no one will even know about my existence, so it really doesn't matter if I'm not 'as good' as someone else, what matters is finding happiness.

When I cook my dinner at night, I know that it's a privilege to be able to choose what to buy and what to eat, but when I'm busy, it's easy to forget and take it for granted. I remind myself that the only person who can feel the stress I'm feeling is me. We all feel stress, but we all have some level of control over the stress we feel. It's our expectations about what our life should be like or how our day should go that cause us stress. If I wake up and tell myself, today I'm going to do a sixty-mile ride, the weather will be good, I'll be home for this time and then cook tea, but then it rains, there's a road closure, so I can't do my full mileage and dinner isn't as nice as I planned it to be, I would probably be annoyed and disappointed, I'd be stressing about the road closure and for not having done my miles. I have control over how I react. I've put the expectations on that day, so I've made the stressors. Instead, I try to set out on a ride, saying, this is what I've planned, but we'll see how it goes and that takes the pressure off and allows me to enjoy my ride more.

One person might get really stressed about burning dinner; another person might say oh well and laugh about it. One person might find their petrol going into the red stressful; another person might be totally unbothered. As you've probably gathered by now, I'm a natural stress pot and I'm guilty of letting things get to me easily. If I'm on a bike ride and I go the wrong way, I don't get stressed. It's part of the adventure, but if I go the wrong way when driving, it's a whole different story! I'm trying to be more reflective and reduce the stress that I feel. Don't get me wrong, I know there are some things that are very stressful and we don't have an off switch to stress. But with minor events like spilling a drink on the carpet or being a little late to work, I'm beginning to think that feeling stress is wasted energy; whether I get stressed about burning dinner or not, the dinner is still burnt. So now, when a minor stressful thing happens, I try to remember it's just minor; everything will work out in the end and my stress will only make things more uncomfortable for me. I sometimes take myself back to the highlands in my mind, back to the little road along the coast that led to Achmelvich youth hostel, back to the yipeee down into Tongue, seeing the youth hostel in the distance over the loch after a long day in the saddle, back to hurdling over cattle grids and snack stops with epic views and my mind feels calm again.

I went to a cafe yesterday; I'd been on a solo ride in the morning, a zone four, push the pedals, go as fast as you can sort of ride and when I got home, Kyle suggested a dog walk and cafe, hearing the word cafe and knowing they do a banging chai latte, I didn't need asking more than once! I had my shoes on ready to go before he heard me say yes; you don't need to ask a cyclist if they want to go to a cafe. When a hard ride is done, food is on the mind.

As I approached the till to make my order, a large chai latte and a mocha for Kyle, I noticed how stressed the waitress looked. Neck flushed, hot and bothered, no eye contact given to anyone, glaring at the screen and eyes flitting from that to the till to the coffee machine behind her. Speaking fast, in a rush to get the queue down and feeling the stress of the Sunday afternoon rush. There's me feeling calm and relaxed, not bothered if I have to wait a little to get served, opposite a lady who looked like she was going to burst with worry over coffee and cakes. I wanted to say, 'It's okay, we can all wait, don't raise your blood pressure for me!' In that moment, it made me realise how much pressure we can put on ourselves and how we have the power to reduce that pressure on ourselves and on each other. The waitress could think, 'Omg, I've got to serve all these people; they're going to start complaining if they have to wait too long, I can't do it' or 'Wow, we're busy today, that's good for the business, might mean a bit of a wait for them but oh well It's just coffee and cake and no one's got anywhere to be on a Sunday.' I try to reframe my stress thoughts like this. It doesn't always work, but now I remind myself of the stressed coffee waitress and it helps a little; no amount of stress can change the situation, but the way you think about it can change your stress levels.

Little mental health tip: You're capable of more than you think; don't let your inner critic stop your dreams.

Everesting

When we got back from Scotland, as usual, I was hungry for the next challenge. We were out on a club ride one Sunday near Beeley Moor and a club mate spoke of when someone they knew 'Everested' on the Beeley Moor climb, "What's Everesting?" I asked with new challenge ideas bubbling inside, "It's where you cycle up and down the same hill until you reach the equivalent height of Everest." Immediately, the cogs in my brain started to whir; it sounded brutal but, at the same time, appealing. I got home, googled it straight away and discovered the Everesting website. There were rules I had to follow if I was going to do it officially and make it onto the Everesting "wall of fame"; 'it must be recorded on strava,' 'it must be in one attempt' so no sleeping, "on one hill", "no loops", making it more monotonous and more of a challenge. It was September at this point, with the end of the year, darker mornings and colder nights approaching. I set a date in October, not giving me much time to prepare, but I was keen to do it before the end of the year and I felt like I had the miles in my legs to do it. I decided to do it to raise money for a suicide prevention mental health charity.

The October day soon came around and with my plan submitted to the Everesting team, off I set at two a.m. in the morning, forty-six times up and down Star Bank Climb in Oakamoor would put me at the height of Everest, eight thousand eight hundred forty-nine meters. The climb was 1.78 miles long and an average gradient of 7.3%. Rain and mist filled the air as I set off into the darkness; Kyle was at the top of the climb, snacks and cheers in good supply and the first ten reps went by in a flash. I stopped for a big tub of porridge and a jersey change as the sun started to rise and the rain came to an end. Throughout the day, cyclists from my club came to do a few reps with me, urging me to keep on pedalling with a smile. The day went on and I continued, grinding up and slowly spinning the legs back down again. A stop for a tuna baguette with Kyle's Grandparents was a nice break; a wee behind a bush with my legs shaking and struggling to hold a squat position was not so nice, I started to wish that Kyle's van was a camper van that had a toilet so I could sit down, maybe I could even have a sleep. Then I snapped out of my moan and reminded myself that I'd been sitting down all day! There was another part of the ride where I started to wonder whether I could fake an injury, so I could stop. Again, I snapped myself out of those thoughts, realistically I'd never let myself quit or fake being in pain, but having the option helped.

There were times in this ride when I felt like giving up, my stomach feeling full with all the food I had to eat, my head feeling heavy, my neck feeling sore and my mind getting bored by the monotonous up and down, seeing the same cows over and over again, the same stones on the road, the sound of my own breathing becoming annoying. But giving up is never an option for me and although parts of the ride were hard, I enjoyed the challenge. A cycling friend, Rebecca, came and did some reps with me just at the right time. I was starting to feel really sick and the thought of how much further I still had to go was getting to me, but her fresh legs and chatter about her experience of doing Ironmans and how many gels she had to eat when doing them passed the time and before I knew it another three laps were done. One of my best friends, Ellie, who doesn't cycle, came to cheer me on and brought me a chocolate milkshake, which I gulped down in no time; the feelings of sickness had luckily passed at this point and her arrival gave my legs another boost.

It started to get dark and with only four laps left to go, I struggled to put on my high-vis strap; fears of "I'm going to get hit by a car" started to invade my mind out of nowhere, but my mum being there calmed me down; she doesn't really like cycling, but she did a rep on my dad's bike as he shouted out to her about one of the gears being dodgy and not to use that one, my mum replying "I know how to use a bike!" My dad did a rep too, although he was slightly more interested in going into the pub across the road! Out of which came a load of people who put money in the donation bucket; my dad had enthusiastically told them about my challenge and they were in disbelief at how many times I'd gone up and down the climb.

With each rep now taking longer as my legs began to tire, at eight p.m., my mum and dad left to go and get a curry ready at home. I was almost at the end now and I pictured the feeling of finishing, imagining how the money I'd raised would help towards providing support sessions for people who needed them. I got to the top of the last rep; Kyle stood waiting for me after having ridden the previous two laps with me to spur me on. Eighteen hours, thirty-one minutes and ten seconds since I started, 8.31 pm. I was ready for the biggest curry ever and a long, warm bath! We got back to my mum and dad's house and I only managed a few mouthfuls; I felt really sick and my breathing was hard; all I wanted to do was go to bed, so I did and had the curry for lunch the next day along with a lot of other food!

It turned out that Kyle had miscounted my reps, so I actually ended up climbing nine thousand six hundred and nineteen meters, seven hundred seventy meters more than I needed to, but I wasn't annoyed at him; we had a laugh about it the next morning, I was just grateful that as always he had been there to support me. I was feeling slightly guilty, but he reassured me that he wanted to be there and that he enjoyed it, he'd rather have been the one giving out the snacks than the one struggling to eat them! The next morning, I surprisingly didn't feel as bad as I expected to and was all for riding a thirty-mile loop to a cafe, but both Kyle and my mum put their foot down, "Amy, you're resting today." So, I reluctantly joined them in the car and we went to the cafe for hot chocolate and flapjacks. I hadn't quite processed the previous day yet, still feeling a little tired and dazed, but I felt proud of myself, something that I rarely feel.

Little mental health tip: Don't let fear stop you from taking opportunities that come your way.

How Did I Get Here?
Italy and France

Since cycling LEJOG and starting Instagramming, my followers somehow started to grow; what started with three hundred followers made up of old school friends and family had soon become ten thousand and by the time I got home from the NC500, twenty thousand, increasing each week. I never expected it to become something; I never expected anyone to care what I was doing, so when I was offered the chance to go to Italy to see the Giro in May 2023 with Santini and France to see a stage of the Tour De France in July 2023, I couldn't believe it. I felt like an imposter and they must have asked the wrong person by accident. Santini is a clothing brand who are stocked in my local bike shop, Velo Bavarian, which I race for (albeit not for long, as I've decided endurance is what I enjoy), so it is through this connection that these opportunities came about. On both of these trips, I'm surprised I didn't come home with a smile permanently stuck on my face. Being up close to pros, soaking in the atmosphere of a tour, bike riding abroad, meeting new people and trying new food, some of these things would have caused me such anxiety before, but with my mind on cycling, I took it all in and enjoyed every moment. I'd never been to Italy before; we stayed in Bergamo, where the Santini HQ is; it's a beautiful place; a tram takes you up to the old town, where narrow streets full of bakeries and little shops bustle with people, stone buildings and cobbled floors. The first day of the trip to Italy involved a ride out to see the Giro; we were given bikes to ride, a trek with Di2 gears, which are electric gears that change with the tap of a finger. I took a moment; how did I get from riding my Carrera in the peak district with my dad to being invited to Italy on a bike with electric gears?! A group of about fourteen of us set off on the ride, taking in the views, tackling the Italian language barrier, sharing smiles and laughs and munching on snacks. Our spot to watch the Giro was at the top of the Roncola climb and my inner mountain goat came out to play; a little bit of determination to try and beat some of the men appeared inside me and off I pedalled as we got to the climb, getting to the top third, I was happy, it wasn't a race, but it kind of was. Jon, the English rep, a real character who had me and Luke (the bike shop director), laughing the whole trip, got to the top and immediately poured his whole bottle of water over his head. He then joined me for a top-of-the-hill dance and later took us out for dinner, where I mistakenly ordered a chic pea soup, which Jon had told me was pasta. Let's just say we need to brush up on our Italian! Day two brought a tour of the Santini factory and it was fabulous, a behind-the-scenes peak at what goes on in cycling clothes production. I felt in my element and didn't want to go home! But I had to accept that home time had come and after some time exploring the old town of Bergamo on day three and getting lost on the way back to HQ in the thirty-degree heat, an emergency magnum was eaten and an Uber called to get us to the airport in time. The little glimpse that I saw of Italy was beautiful and it's definitely a place I want to return to.

The Tour De France was another level up; a ride out on the first day was just the warm-up, there was me and Luke from England and the rest of the group was French; the language barrier wasn't too much of an issue, though, we picked up a bit of French "tournez a droit" turn right, "tournez a Gouch" turn left, I don't think I'll be fluent anytime soon! We cycled up Col de Cessat and I did my usual top-of-the-hill dance at the top, much to the amusement of the French men who wondered what on earth I was doing. We freewheeled back down and had an afternoon of playing boule in the garden; I thought they were calling me Julie, but they were, in fact, saying "bien joué", which means well done. I had to keep pinching myself to make sure this was happening. We stayed in one of the nicest houses I've ever seen, with shutters on the windows, stone floors, a view across the mountains, a garden with two chickens (I do love my animals!), a pool, a large table with pink and blue umbrellas where breakfast of pancakes, croissants, chocolate cake (even with my sweet tooth I couldn't stomach having cake for breakfast) and fresh juice awaited each morning.

The main event of the trip was watching stage ten of the Tour De France. I really did feel like an imposter; from the start, the day was a buzz of activity and excitement. We walked through the rider area and I almost walked into Tom Pidcock and got a picture with Peter Sagan (people that I never knew existed prior to my new hobby becoming my life). This was followed by a rush back to the Santini car, where we drove the route of the riders, waving to TDF fans who had painted faces, flags, bottles of beer, camper vans and massive smiles, to the top of a climb. Here, we were given a lunch bag each. To my delight, a crunchy apple was part of the pack and we saw the riders whip past a flying speed. I grabbed a polka-dot hat and then we rushed back to the car. We drove again, taking the route the riders would soon come through rural France, greenery all around and more people with camper vans. I imagined what it would be like to be a Tour de France rider; I bet they don't see any of the scenery, eyes focused on the wheel in front, mind focused on a win or whatever their role is in their team, looking for the break, chasing the break-away, miles of scenery lost to miles of racing. We rushed to the next spot and sat on a bridge, eagerly awaiting the return of the riders, hearing the filming helicopter above followed by the passing of motorbikes and distant cheers signalled their arrival; the riders flew past us so close we were almost knocked off the wall! In touching reach of riding legends, they went by so fast I couldn't make out who was who, flashes of red, green and blue kits, I could just about make out the teams. Some cold drinks were offered around as the sun heated us up to thirty-five degrees and then we headed to the finish to cheer on the riders on their final few miles. The day was a dream come true and one I will never forget, the yellow Tour De France signs imprinted in my mind. We ended the trip with the best meal I've ever tasted in Clermont Ferrand; it truly was a dream trip filled with excitement and the buzz of the tour, one that I will remember and feel grateful for forever.

I'm so grateful for everything cycling has brought my way. I kept having to take a minute to make sure these trips were real. I never thought things like this would happen to me and part of me couldn't accept that I deserved it. Leading up to and after the trips, I felt like other people deserved it more or might say, how come you get to go and do that? And my response would be, "I don't know, maybe I shouldn't get to". But then I think about all the hours of work that goes into my social media that no one really knows about other than Kyle; when I started, it was just a bit of fun and I never realised what work it took to keep it going, I'm in no way complaining because I actually really enjoy documenting my rides, it's nice to look back on even if no one else watches! I was never very popular at school, feeling like I didn't fit in, feeling like everyone judged me and thought I was weird (I am weird, we all are!), so when I get messages saying, "I've started cycling after watching your video, you're an inspiration to me" it shocks me because I don't see myself as inspirational, there are far far far more inspirational people in cycling than me, I'm just a woman who rides her bike. But it fills me with happiness to hear about more people giving cycling a go and that's why I spend so much of my free time putting cycling content out there because without cycling, I don't know where I'd be and if cycling can do the same for just one other person, then that's someone else's life that's still here.

Little mental health tip: Do something nice for someone you love with today; reach out and tell them how much they mean to you.

Cycling for Twenty-Four Hours

I love a challenge and in July 2023, I did my first ever time trial, the national twenty-four-hour time trial. I signed up for the event at the end of June; it had been mentioned to me a few times by various club members, including Nige and Jim Hopper. I was introduced to Jim by Nige at Derby Mercury Road Club and we often cycle over to see him now. I'm actually planning on cycling over to Jim's next week, I need to return his PBP high vis he gave to me in the night in the middle of the twenty-four-hour TT when I was feeling a little cold and the road was feeling very dark. Don't worry, I had my bike lit up like a Christmas tree, but the brighter you can be, the better, so I took the high-vis with open arms whilst getting a few porridge pots down me during a quick break. Jim's house has framed records all over the walls and he always likes to have a chat with a cuppa, re-telling tales we've heard before, but we don't mind; it's nice to spend time with him and I always feel guilty when we leave, as he's on his own. He emailed me the other day: "Just a note to say thanks. This morning, we fell in with some Tamworth CC. I was asked if I was the chap on Amy's YouTube. After all these years, fame has found me…it is worth waiting for." Cycling really is his life and he's done some amazing rides. So, feeling

Jimspired, when I got home from a ride out to see him, I booked the twenty-four-hour TT whilst sat watching Love Island.

I rode my bike from 1.28 pm on a Saturday afternoon to 1.28 pm on Sunday, with a total of one hour forty minutes of stops for kit changes and whacking down as much food as I could: porridge pots, pasta, rice, energy bars, Kendal mint cake to name a few. The weather was awful; it rained for about twenty hours of the ride and there was a fair bit of wind as well. But I LOVED it; I smiled my way past the Marshalls and supporters as they cheered me along, feeling so at peace with my mind and grateful that I could ride my bike without any intrusive thoughts invading. Jim was there the whole time, giving me words of encouragement as I whipped my go-pro out to capture some action: "You've not got time for that get pedalling" and "Come on, you can average eighteen mph now", as I'd just been sick! But he made me laugh and I could tell he was loving being part of it.

Before I set off on the ride, my mind was full of doubts, 'I can't do this' and there'd been multiple times leading up to the ride where I'd said, 'I'm not doing it', but I never let self-doubt stop me and I'd already paid the £50 entry fee so off I went. As soon as I started pedalling, my worries faded; all I had to do was pedal and keep pedalling; riding my bike is what I love to do. Kyle was my support man, along with a few other members of the Derby Mercury Road Club; when we arrived, Kyle pinned my number on my back; this took a few attempts, including a few safety pins being bent! I rolled down to the start point and joined my place in the queue behind number twenty-seven. At 1.28, it was my time to go; a ten second countdown and off I was sent; it all felt very official; I was just there for a long ride; I didn't have the aero-helmet or TT bike; I just wanted to see how far I could do, my only competition was myself. Kyle waved me off from the start line and shouted good luck, a massive smile exchanged as I struggled to get my foot clipped into the pedal and set off in the stiffest gear as I always do. Then I calmed myself down and followed the Marshalls, who directed me left at the first junction I came to. The first few hours went past in a blink, my body full of adrenaline at the idea of a challenge, my mind alert and motivated, fuelled by the idea of completing my biggest challenge. It wasn't my usual choice of a scenic ride, a main road with cars flying past, but I didn't really notice them too much; my mind was full of excitement for the challenge and with so many other riders in front and behind me, I felt safe. Kyle and the crew set up a gazebo on the roadside next to all the other supporters who were also on snack and kit change duty; each time I rode past (every thirty or fifteen miles, depending on the circuit I was directed onto), I would shout out what I wanted next time. The rain was biblical; I might as well have worn a wetsuit, but there's something about riding in the rain that I quite like; it makes you feel alive and in some of my darkest times, I craved rides in the rain to feel less numb. Luckily, it wasn't cold, but I needed to change the kit a few times and layer up for the night.

Riding at night is something I've always been a bit scared of, but at this event, with other riders on the road and knowing that Marshalls or Kyle were close by, fear wasn't being let in. There were about seventy riders altogether, nine of which were women. Every so often, I would pass by another rider, or they would pass by me; this would always give me a little boost and I made an effort to cheer them along. With each lap, my mindset changed a little bit; the thirty-mile laps went by quickly at first but felt longer as the hours went on. I used the next Marshalls as motivation; seeing other people and getting a little cheer was a big mood boost. There was a kid shouting 'come on, let's 'av' it' that always gave me a smile and another man who said 'well-done rider' each time I passed, as I approached him each time I waited for him to say it, a little more motivation to keep the legs spinning. One lap in the night, my eyes wanted to close and I had to sing out loud to myself to keep my focus and not let them shut. The worst lap of all was at about one a.m. I was sick a few times, the amount of food I had to eat churning inside me as my body struggled to digest while I was on the move, as I leant over and spewed on the grass, I started to question why I was doing it and as I got back on the bike thought about why; to prove that I'm not just a 'cycling influencer' as people so often said I was (this doesn't feel real to me!), to prove that I can do hard things, because I love the element of challenge and in a way maybe to feel worthy, I wasn't doing it for other people, I was doing it for me. After this tough lap, I had a fifteen minutes sit-down and spoke to myself in my head, "Come on, Amy, you can do this", "you've been through much harder things than this in your head" and "Just get on with it and blooming enjoy it!" I got back on the bike again, determined not to give up; there was no pressure to continue; everyone who loves me would love me the same whether I finished or not; I could say, "That's enough. I'm done." whenever I wanted, but that thought never crossed my mind, that wasn't an option and I didn't want to give up, I wanted to finish. A quick banana down my gullet and I felt good to go. I don't know what happened on the next lap, but I felt amazing: two a.m. in the morning, pitch black all around me apart from my bike light illuminating the road and I was buzzing. I sang myself around the thirty miles, 'I like to ride my bicycle', 'whooaaahhhh! We're halfway there' was blurted out when I reached the twelve-hour mark and some random songs I made up in my head, waving and shouting enthusiastically "you got this", "keep going", "yeaaaa" to the cyclists on the other side of the road as we passed, most of them probably wondering what on earth I was so cheery about in the rain halfway through the ride. Kyle and the crew looked shocked when I came back around smiling. And my smile never really faded after this point. I just felt so happy. I rode around reflecting on the past few years, how my life hasn't taken the path I thought it would, how financially I'm not where I wanted to be, I don't earn a lot of money, but I'm so much happier. I never expected to find a hobby that I love so much and that brings me so much joy. I can't explain the feeling it gives me; it's almost like an addiction, but a good addiction. So, I rode with a smile, cheering on the other riders because I felt grateful to be in the moment I was in, riding in the rain without worries.

My aim was to ride six hundred km and I rode six hundred thirty-four km, three hundred ninety-four miles. I rode on my Canyon Endurace road bike, or as I like to call her, 'Canny', finishing third female. The final finishing circuit was full of supporters cheering us on and the atmosphere was awesome; the sun came out and it was as if the positive energy of the new supporters, who looked fresh after a night's sleep, diffused into my loins and gave me a final burst of energy. Although my bum was in pain (let's just say a certain pair of cycling bib-shorts will not be worn again), I was nearly at the end, so I focused on getting final miles in and got up off the saddle as much as I could to prevent the pain. Then, finally, before I knew it, twenty-four hours had passed. I pedalled to the next checkpoint, where Marshalls marked the end of my ride and there Kyle was waiting for me with his van, face beaming. I gently got off the bike and straight away said, "I'm doing that again next year." I got lots of strange looks in response. Apparently, I should never want to do it again! I surprisingly didn't feel too shattered. Instead, I felt high with happiness and my original plan to sleep on the one-and-a-half-hour drive home went out the window; I was wide awake. Wide awake and bursting with energy, the opposite of how I thought I'd feel. We went back to the village hall and I had a shower in the men's changing room, which had the lovely additional extra of grass, mud-tinged with the smell of a sweaty PE changing room, but I didn't care; it felt so nice to take the sweaty Lycra off, I carefully tiptoed to the shower, avoiding the muddy clumps on the floor, freshened up and whacked on some comfy baggy clothes. Then, we waited as the results were put up. They missed one of my laps, so I was put down at three hundred eighty-one miles (this has since been corrected to three hundred ninety-four) and I was shocked to find out that I had come third woman. I didn't enter thinking I'd get a top three place and winning was never a motivation for me; it was about the personal achievement, proving to myself that I can do what I put my mind to and that I'm not a failure, trying to pedal that feeling that sits deep within me away.

Little mental health tip: Spend some time outdoors today without distraction. Just spending a bit of time in nature can make a big difference; look up at the sky, notice the birds and hear the wind. (I take my dog on his walk each morning with my phone on aeroplane mode, so I can't get distracted).

Smelling Cinnamon

The other day, I made some walnut, apple and cinnamon cakes; if I say so myself, they're a great snack after a bike ride or during it if you can fit them in your jersey pocket! I mixed together a thick, gooey, sugary mixture of cinnamon goodness. I sliced apples into the smallest chunks I could, chopped walnuts in half, mixed them in and baked the goo into fluffy, warm cakes. When I took them out of the oven, after the wave of warmth hit my face, I had one or maybe two. The soft texture, the smell of cinnamon and the warmth that burst out of them was so comforting; I wanted to stay in that moment for as long as I could. It reminded me that it's the small things that make a difference. It's the small things we have to treasure.

When I walked into the house after taking Chester for a walk half an hour later, the cinnamon smell was still floating in the air and embraced me in from the cold, tempting me to have another. Whenever I smell cinnamon, I feel at home and the cinnamon cupcakes are now my go-to comfort recipe. It's noticing the simplest things like this that can make a massive difference to your mood.

Being grateful for the little things is something that has really helped me mentally. I try to think of two things I'm grateful for every day (I'm human, so I often forget to do it!) because it reminds me that there are good things happening all the time and not to take things for granted. I've actually got a really bad cold at the minute; I'm writing this feeling annoyed that I'm not well enough to go on the bike ride I planned. But one thing's for sure: I'm not going to take a day without a headache or use of a tissue for granted again; once I can breathe properly again, that will be one of the things I'm grateful for that day. Today, I'm grateful for my Chester, who's been lying by me all day and keeping me company and for oranges because they're tasty and hopefully, the vitamin C will be helping fight this cold!

Little mental health tip: Reframe 'failures' as learning events; it's better to try and 'fail' than to not try at all. There is something to be learned from things not going as planned.

Failure Shows You're Trying and Mistakes Are Okay

It's completely okay to fail at something; in fact, it can be a good thing. You might be thinking, what on earth is this girl on about? But you can't fail unless you're trying something, so don't be hard on yourself. It's so easy to jump to the negatives and put yourself down, but if you dropped your phone on the floor and the screen smashed, would you stamp on it to smash it even more? If your friend failed an exam, would you tell them to give up trying? Two no's (I hope). So, instead of beating yourself up, pick yourself back up and try again. View any 'failures' as something to learn from; you haven't failed, you've just learnt that this time it didn't work and maybe there's a different way to try next time.

I wish I could imprint the above paragraph into my brain. I wrote it, but it doesn't mean I can apply it. I believe it and I want to be able to live my life thinking that way, but it's not as easy as writing it out or reading it and it suddenly being the way you live. If it was, life would be easy. But I'm working on it and the more I read it, the more it sinks in and the more determined I am to live my life, not letting 'failures' rule over me. After all, one person's idea of failure is completely different to anyone else's; it's subjective. So, when I don't get the percentage I want on a finance exam or don't hit the speed I want to on a ride, I remind myself it's only my brain's version of a failure, no one else and I have the power to decide that it's not a failure. I can remember when I was studying to be a nurse, we had a blood pressure exam where we had to take manual blood pressure and pulse and be watched doing it. I had already convinced myself that I was going to fail as I wasn't very confident with manual blood pressure; I always seemed to let the air out too soon and miss the systolic reading. I walked into the fake scenario and started with the pulse, two fingers on the lady's wrist, searched for the beat and tried to focus on counting that whilst being able to feel my own heartbeat pulsing blood through my body wasn't ideal; my nerves getting the better of me, written exams, not a problem but being watched doing something, no thank you. But the pulse was correct and I moved on to the next part, the manual blood pressure. I tried about five times, getting more worked up each time; I couldn't see the beat, so I had to give my best guess, which was wrong. I walked out of the room, failure circling around in my head. It was okay as I could just re-do the exam next week, not a problem really, other people failed too. But to me, it was the worst thing ever at that time; I was so hard on myself; I literally spent every night for the next week worrying and all my spare time doing everyone's blood pressure. I knew my parents, Kyle's, sisters and Gran's blood pressure off by heart by the end of the week. My mind told me that I would fail again and

I knew that if I did fail again, I wouldn't be allowed into year two of the degree...in hindsight, maybe if I failed again, it would have saved me from going down a career path that wasn't for me! But the second time around, I passed and all my doubt was flushed away with the tick of a pen and a "well done" from the examiner.

One thing that's taken me forever to accept and I admit I still don't always accept, is that it's okay to make a mistake. When I make a mistake, it's like the mini police in my brain have a meltdown – 'You're stupid', 'You're worthless', 'See, you shouldn't even bother trying', ' You mess everything up'. These thoughts could pop up over the slightest of things; I might have spilt a cup of water or forgotten to buy something from the shop and I would be hit with a barrage of abuse from myself. The worst thing about these thoughts is that it feels like you can't escape them!

But now that I'm trying out the 'mistakes are something to learn from' concept, if I spill a drink of water (which happens quite often, but it's usually Chester knocking it over rather than me!), I try to look on the bright side; at least I was remembering to drink water for once, I can just fill the glass back up again, no need for drama. If I forget to buy something, oh well, I can either go back to the shop, or I can survive without it until I go again. I say to myself, 'Mistakes make me human' and try to repeat this to myself calmly. Of course, this doesn't always work; there will always be times when we get annoyed about something we've done and wish we'd done something differently. Luckily, when I'm in a positive mindset, which seems to be happening more often, I just say oh blooming heck, get over it and carry on with my day, smiling my way through it because life is way too short to get wound up over something you won't remember in a years' time.

Little mental health tip: Try talking to yourself the way you would talk to a friend. If we talked to friends the way we spoke to ourselves, I don't think we'd have many friends.

Hope

The number one thing that keeps us all going. Without hope, what do we have?

If we didn't have hope, would we do the hard things?

Would we keep going when times are tough?

I recently read *A River in Darkness*, which details the tragic life of a man who lived in North Korea. His strength to keep going through all the terrible things he's lived through shows the pure power of hope when all humanity is lost. I read in disbelief at what he's been through and a big part of me felt very guilty for ever feeling low. But that's the thing with mental illness: it doesn't matter how great a life you have; it doesn't have any conditions on who it affects.

I feel so lucky to have the life I have and I have to admit that, at times, I take it for granted. I rush through my day not appreciating the little moment of happiness, getting wound up about things that don't really matter, like the pile of ironing that needs doing, running out of milk or crumbs on the worktop. I have to bring myself back into the moment sometimes and remind myself of how great life is now that I don't have intrusive thoughts ruining every moment. On the days when my mind went into meltdown and I felt like the worst human ever, it was hope that kept me going. I had hope that things would get better; I had hope that my mind would settle. I hoped for better days, even when I didn't believe they would arrive. If I didn't have hope, I think I would have given up. I don't know where hope comes from, but it seems to be from within. I think it's made more powerful by those around you. Part of my hope came from family and as I have gotten better, the hope has come more and more from within myself. And now I'm at a place where I'm not hoping for better days because the better days are here.

Little mental health tip: It's not until it's gone that you realise how good it is.

600 KM Ride
Qualifying for Paris-Brest-Paris

It was May 2023 and I had completed my two-hundred km, three-hundred km and four hundred km qualifying rides for Paris-Brest-Paris (PBP). There was just the six-hundred km ride left and then I would be all set to head to Paris in August. To qualify for PBP, you must complete the four-distance Audax's during certain time frames, set out by Audax, during the year of the event. The six-hundred km ride had been the one I was very nervous about because it would be my longest ride yet (this ride was before the twenty-four-hour TT in July '23).

On 12 May 2023, Kyle and I drove down to Tewksbury after work, staying in a B&B the night before the 600 km (Benjamin Allen's Summer Outing Audax) to avoid a stupidly early drive down in the morning to start the ride. Kyle couldn't do the ride with me as we didn't have dog-sitters available, so we agreed that I'd do this one and he booked his 600 km in for June, when I would have finance exams to be focusing on. I was gutted about this as having him by my side always makes me feel safer on a ride. But being the hero he is, he wouldn't let me drive down on my own and insisted on coming with me to wave me off, before heading home with the Chester and then making the trip back to pick me up when I was finished.

The whole week before this ride, my anxiety was getting the better of me; the furthest I'd ridden before this was 400 km and my mind was running away with worst-case scenarios, stressing that I'd get a mechanical in the middle of the night, have no signal, not be able to fix it, be left in the cold and then potentially get abducted – welcome to an overthinking mind! But I went prepared with all my tools (packed in a trusty Carridace saddlebag borrowed from a fellow Audaxer), bright lights, high-vis jacket and I told myself that whatever problems came my way I would get through them, "So, stop worrying about things that haven't happened and the things you can't control, because every Audax you've done so far you've loved." (I did spend a good couple of hours practicing puncture fixing the week before).

My alarm went off at four a.m., a porridge pot with banana made in the B&B bedroom was the pre-ride breakfast and off we drove ten minutes down the road to a little car park in Tewksbury where the ride started. Still pitch black, at four thirty a.m., there was a little bubble of tired but determined-looking cyclists, talking under hushed voices in the early morning so as not to disturb any residents. Bikes were awash with bags. High-vis jackets were the clothing of choice. Last-minute snacks were consumed, I took three or four trips to the public toilet before I set off, just to make sure and Kyle took a quick picture of me with my Brevet before I set off at five a.m. A wave from Kyle, the same wave he gave me when I set out on my first long solo ride home from Wales, and I was off. But this time, I wasn't alone, there was a whole bunch of other crazy cyclists along for the ride too.

Only a few miles into the ride I was already loving it, the sun rising was like a warm hug, the road ahead of me littered with red lights and with the sound of wheel hubs whirring. I found myself riding along in a bunch and had an immediate sense of "everything will be okay." It was a beautiful day; blue sky, rolling roads, green fields, waving to cows and horses, snack top-ups at co-ops, a café lunch, sweating up climbs and freewheeling back down, "hello" echoed with passing cyclists, I was in my element and loving every second.

About ten miles into the ride, I met Rob, who was also aiming for PBP qualification. We agreed to ride to the 400 km sleep control at Wigmore together; my anxiety was instantly lessened, my fear of getting stranded in the dark alone diminished and I could enjoy myself. We got through the first 400 km in good spirits, some sections in silence just enjoying the views, or breathless from tackling the climbs, other points chatting the miles away. Rob told me about how he completed a 1200 km ride last year called London–Edinburgh–London and this gave me another ride to add to my to-do list. Control points were a great way to break the mileage down and the food that came with them was an extra motivation; we stopped at a café in Llandovery for lunch, where we got a stamp on our brevet cards. Rob opted for a cottage pie while I had the biggest plate of beans on toast I've ever seen! Between more green scenery and warm sun control points, we ticked off the mileage happily. I was breaking down the total distance in my mind to the distance between each control point, which made it seem more manageable. At one control, a village shop, the sun was beating down and we were feeling the heat. Out came a very flushed-looking rider in a long-sleeve top and leggings. He was regretting his decision as he bought ice cream and litre bottles of water to cool down. The final food stop of the day was at a McDonalds in Newtown; chicken nuggets and a hot choc went down a treat before cycling in the dark up the biggest climb of the day, then carefully descending down into Wigmore. Most people would have been sat at home watching *Eurovision* and there we were cycling into the night! No wonder everyone I work with looks at me with complete disbelief when they ask me what I did over the weekend; it's not normal for the non-cycling crew, but I wouldn't want to spend my weekend any other way. If I'm not at work, you'll find me on the bike.

We arrived at the 400 km control point, a village hall in Wigmore, just after twelve a.m. with Rob exclaiming that he'd just done his fastest ever two-hundred, three-hundred and four-hundred km rides. We left our bikes around the back with the others that were there and were greeted with friendly faces from volunteers who dished out pasta and cake for us. Airbeds and blankets were set up in the village hall to sleep. I initially planned to sleep for four hours, but I just couldn't settle and the road was pulling me back out to ride. I got an hour and a half of sleep and then decided the snoring from other riders wasn't going to stop, so off I rode solo into the mist at 2.40 a.m. with 200 km to go. Although my legs were pedalling faster (due to fear) the 76 km ride to the petrol station control in Allensmore seemed to last forever. I was proud of myself to be facing my fear of riding in the dark on my own, but knowing the sun would rise was a great motivation. I've only ridden in the dark a handful of times and it's something I know I need to get used to if I want to do more endurance riding. Don't get me wrong, daytime riding is my preference but on this ride, I discovered that there's something eerily nice about riding in the dark; seeing the world from a different angle, senses heightened to the night-time nature and a sense of fear mixed with motivation to reach the next destination made the legs spin a little faster. I rolled into the petrol station with porridge on my mind, but wow, what a snack selection I was greeted with; homemade cakes, flapjacks, tiffin and even samosas, not quite a five a.m. snack but they went in the Carradice bag for later and I managed to nab the last porridge pot they had, which filled a hole for now. I met another cyclist here who had been riding without a sleep stop; it amazes me how people do this!

With 125 km to go, the thrill of night riding came to an end as the sun rose, but it was still misty and cold (I couldn't complain after yesterday's glorious weather, though) and I realised that borrowing my dad's saddle to be able to attach the Carradice to was not a good idea. Let's just say, soreness set in and I won't be making that mistake again! After passing through the beautiful Wye Valley which filled me with memories of LEJOG last year, feeling disappointed that the public toilet was closed and not finding a gate or bush to nip behind, I met the cyclist from the petrol station again and riding along with him distracted me from my discomfort on the saddle and desperate need for a wee! As we cycled over the Severn bridge, perky Sunday social riders were setting off on their rides. I cycled with a smile and a wave, wishing I had their energy and wondering how far they would ride today. Nearing the end of the route, feeling a sense of relief that soon I would be able to get off the uncomfortable saddle, whilst at the same time not wanting the ride to end, we bumped along a canal path and got through a very packed Gloucester before arriving back into Tewksbury, just before twelve p.m., thirty-one hours after I set off the day before for the final stamp on our brevets. Kyle was there waiting for me with Chester, who excitedly jumped up, nearly knocking me off my bike. My body was tired, but my mind was full of happiness. I headed home with a sense of accomplishment, feeling grateful to be part of such a supportive community, glad to have proved my anxiety wrong, excited for Paris-Brest-Paris and ready to demolish a very big Sunday dinner

Paris–Brest–Paris, My Biggest Bike Challenge Yet

Bloomin-heck, I've been writing this book so long I've done Paris–Brest–Paris now! I got home yesterday and I have to share the experience; it was by far the best and hardest bike ride I've done so far. As I've said before, it only happens every four years, so when I read about it in a cycling book while on my honeymoon in 2022, with it being one and half years away, I suddenly found a challenge to aim for. It's strange to think that when I read that book, sat on a sandy beach in St Lucia (dream holiday alert), I wasn't part of a cycling club; the furthest I'd ridden in a day was one hundred sixty miles (257.5km) and I'd never ridden an Audax, but once I get my mind on something, there's no stopping me.

Fast forward to August 2023, seventeen Audax's later and we were heading to France. Me, Kyle, with some very large panniers and four other members of Derby Mercury Cycling Club, with the club bugle in tow, which Nige tried to make a note out of to sound our arrival and departure at each place we arrived at on the way to and from PBP, some sort of ancient cycling tradition that made quite good entertainment! We boarded the ferry at Portsmouth on a Wednesday night. It was a bit of a rush to get there after being at work in the morning, but we made it, meeting the rest of the club at the Ship and Castle pub for a quick bit of food and, for the men, a few pints. We boarded the ferry, where we met other cyclists also heading for PBP, as well as a man with a fully loaded bike who was heading for a three-month solo cycling trip across the Alps. Bikes were loaded onto the ferry, locked together and our little cabin was found; a quick sleep was had and we woke up the next morning in Caen. Nige (aka the road captain as we called him, who had done PBP twice before) sounded the club bugle as we left the dock and we rode for eighty miles to get to Everoux, a great way to warm up the cod loins (aka the legs) and relax into the journey. Crossing the Pegasus Bridge and stopping off at St Desir war memorial to pay our respects, Nige led the way and told us tales of PBP, littered with advice of taking it steady, making sure to stop to say hi to the children that would come out and cheer us on along the way and reminding us that it's not a race. We lapped up the French roads, passing massive farmhouses with shutters on their windows, rolling on roads that stretch as far as you can see and stopping off at boulangeries. Kyle took a particular liking to Jambon Baguettes and I enjoyed French pastries. Our lunch stop was in Bernay and a tuna salad topped off with a Fanta lemon was beautiful. We stayed in a B&B (Greet hotel) in Everoux that only cost £40 a night with breakfast; as someone who likes to save money whilst also enjoying comforts like a bed and nice bathroom, this was right up my street! It welcomed cyclists with open arms; there were handlebars on the walls and cycling pictures all over the place. The reception had a jar full of chocolate toffees, which I immediately spotted and a handful went in the jersey pocket for the next day's ride. We went out for dinner in the square and I sat there thinking, in seven nights time, I'll be back here and I'll have ridden PBP; I wonder how I'll feel. I really had no clue how I'd feel, but I hoped that I would have enjoyed myself and that all six of us would finish.

The next day, we rode sixty miles to Rambouillet and the PBP excitement really started; we rolled up to a beautiful Chateau to pick up our brevet cards (you get stamps at control points along the way on an Audax to prove you've done the ride, it's handed in at the end to be validated, losing your brevet card is the worst imaginable, so keep it close by at all times!) and numbers for our bikes. The scenic start point with a courtyard and beautiful old buildings was a bit different from the usual village hall starts at Audax's I've done before. Suddenly, it felt real: in two days' time, we were going to cycle twelve hundred km in eighty-four hours; my mind started to throw some doubts in, 'You're not good enough to do this', 'you won't finish,', 'everyone will think you're rubbish', but I quickly tossed those thoughts away and told myself, 'You will finish, there's no other option'. There were cyclists everywhere, all full of excitement, with yellow PBP bags on their backs, all looking at each other, itching to talk to one another, asking where each other was from, what group you would be riding in, the question on everyone's tongue "are you nervous?" of course we are!

With brevets, bike numbers and high-vis jackets collected, we headed to Huttopia, where we stayed for the next few nights, as well as the night after PBP. It was like a cyclist's hub there, with bikes and Lycra-clad people everywhere. We unloaded our stuff into the log cabin. Kyle was especially relieved to take the massive panniers off his bike and head to the bar for pizza. We met cyclists from home as well as America, Australia, Germany and Austria, all looking a little nervous and sharing their ride plans, seeking reassurance from others that it sounded okay, asking what kit others had brought, should we take an extra layer or will we be okay? Some planned to ride six hundred km before stopping to sleep, some didn't plan to sleep but said they would just stop when they got tired, some planned to sleep during the day while it was hot and there were plans of taking as much time as possible and enjoying it, plans of hitting a certain time, plans of just finishing and not caring about the time frame. Mine and Kyle's plan was to stick together no matter what, take in the experience, sleep every four hundred km and, of course, have lots of snacks and laughs along the way.

The first night sleeping in the log cabin, the heat of France hit us and I had to have a cold shower in the night to cool down; Kyle resorted to sticking his head in the freezer, at which point I found a pack of ice cubes which were like a lifesaver. We woke up the next morning, sweaty messes but with excitement about us, 'Tomorrow we will ride PBP!' it still didn't quite feel real, all the build-up, one and half years of having this aim and tomorrow it was actually happening. After breakfast, my usual bowl of porridge and a bit of fruit, I had a sinking feeling as the all too familiar stomach cramps started to happen; a trip to the toilet confirmed it: my period was here; what perfect timing. There was nothing I could do about it. PBP with the accompaniment of Mother Nature was in store, but I didn't let it dampen my spirits; tampons were added into the frame bag and we were good to go. We had a little ride into Rambouillet to cheer off some of the eighty and ninety-hour groups; the atmosphere was hard to describe; stress was in the air coupled with a sense of urgency at wanting to get going and a buzz of 'this is actually happening!'. We cheered off some riders, not quite believing that in the morning, we would be one of them. We found a little bakery and had a strawberry tart as we watched cyclists head to the start; having a moment of calm amongst the rush, Kyle started to say that he felt nervous and didn't know if he was fit enough. I told him that he was beyond fit enough; he's put the miles in at home and is one of the most headstrong people I know, so I had no doubt that he would finish. We took a slow ride back to our hut to have a big bowl of rice and an early night, feeling ready for the three thirty a.m. get up and watching the last few ninety-hour group cyclists free wheel out of the campsite.

The morning came and it felt like we hadn't slept. Pitch black outside, we added in last-minute snacks to our saddle bags and got an early breakfast down us, a big bowl of porridge and a jambon baguette each squished in our back pocket for the road. I was full of excitement and nerves, checking over my bike, making sure whatever I had just put in my top tube bag was still in there and hadn't, by some miracle, vanished. Triple checking that I had my brevet card with me, empty pages that in just over three days' time would hopefully be filled with stamps. I spent time wondering whether I needed the extra layer I had packed or not, deciding it was better to have it than not, a decision I later regretted as the heat hit us. We had eighty-four hours to complete the ride and with all our qualifying rides done and everything packed on our bikes, we were as ready as we could be, heading into the experience full of excitement and nerves and with no real clue what was ahead. It never crossed my mind that we wouldn't finish because I was as determined as ever and I knew if we didn't finish, I'd have an uncomfortable feeling until 2027 when the event was on again.

We rolled in the dark, bike lights illuminating the road, down to Rambouillet, more and more cyclists coming into view as we went. We arrived at the starting village, lights creating a glow around the tent where the first official stamp was secured on our brevets. Then we waited on the start line. I ate my baguette as a distraction from the nerves and Kyle ran over the field to the toilet for a last-minute wee while I held his bike, which was a lot lighter without the panniers on it but still weighed a fair bit with its steel frame and sleeping bag and snacks in tow. Loud music was playing from a stage where a presenter spoke words of encouragement; Happy Birthday was sung to a rider whose fiftieth birthday was today, a strange party sort of atmosphere was created and I had a little dance at the start to warm my loins up, a start of PBP dance instead of a top of the hill one. There was a big digital clock displaying the time and with ten seconds to go, a countdown started; five thirty in the am hit and off we set into the darkness, spurred on by the cyclists around us like a swarm of fireflies lighting up the road as we rode along in a bunch, chasing the sunrise. There were over six thousand riders in the event, one hundred eighty of which set off at the same time as us; more riders continued to leave after us in fifteen-minute intervals. As an early bird, the thought of starting the ride in the evening with the ninety-hour group didn't fill me with optimism, so we opted for the eighty-four-hour morning group, with lots of fireflies ahead; it was a motivation to keep moving forward.

We decided to split the ride into three lots of four hundred km in our minds as this made it seem more manageable. We planned to get a bit of sleep at the end of the first two four hundred km sections and then collapse in a tired heap at the end! People who have done the ride before explained to us how much of an epic atmosphere there is, but you don't understand it until you do it. It really is a festival of cycling; every village had French people out

218

cheering you on, some with food and water stalls offering free pick-me-ups. The famous pancake stall in Saint-Berthevin-La-Tanniere where free pancakes with homemade jam are offered out in return for you sending them a postcard back when you get home. At the top of a climb, there were children with smiles bigger than Kyle's panniers cheering us on; one stop off brought kids with water guns who sprayed us in the face, a welcome treat in the thirty-degree heat and they asked, *"Un bonbon de glacier?"* Knowing that bonbon meant sweet, I nodded with a *"Oui, s'il vous plait"* and a *"merci beaucoup"* as mints were placed in our hands by a girl who must have been six years old, with a smile and excitement that came with that age (the mints came in very handy for the morning breath!). I felt sorry for one child who stood halfway down a descent with a notebook held out for autographs; it was too late for me to stop after I spotted him. It was these people who kept me going when it got hard. Riding along knowing that you were amongst thousands of other cyclists with the same aim of finishing created a community feeling that is hard to describe; a fellow rider giving you a smile, cheer or wince of pain in agreement reminded you that you're not alone. We were all in it together, whilst at the same time all facing individual challenges and circumstances and having to use our own mental strength to face what came our way.

One woman from my club had to pull out due to a bike mechanical; I saw a man with a bad heat stroke who had to stop and one man pulled his back the day before the event but struggled on to Brest (six hundred km) before having to pull out, one man aiming to finish in the quickest time burnt himself out and had to stop at Brest. There were people from all over the world, some on fast carbon bikes, some on steel, some on old bikes with downtube gear shifters, any bike you can imagine we saw it, including velomobiles and even a rider who rode with a delivery bag on his back, which he slept in, yes that's true I'm not making it up! Some people were going as fast as they could, viewing it as a race with support vehicles helping them along the way with fuel and fluid top-ups; they didn't stop at the little village stalls but instead focused on time, whereas some people were trying to get as close to the time limit as possible taking it slow (known as a full value Audax), some people were pushing themselves to make it within the time limit, some people didn't make the time but still carried on (true heroes!), everyone had different aims but what I learnt is that no one but yourself cares how long it takes you and for me, it was about the experience rather than the time, I went with a little aim in my mind but as soon as I saw the true magnitude of the event and when the thirty degree heat hit, any aims for a time went out the window and the only aim was to finish having taken in as much as I could; high fiving the kids, stopping for food breaks and sleeping under the stars. I told myself that I would keep going even if the time limit ran out; in my mind, completing was the only option and me and Kyle finishing together would happen no matter what.

The ride was a challenge; I'd never ridden somewhere so hot and the most I'd ever ridden in one go was six hundred thirty km during the twenty-four-hour time trial. It felt like I was constantly trying to stay on top of preventing sunburn and dehydration whilst trying to manage the stomach cramps that my period brought; the hot flushes I usually experience at that time of the month were made ten times worse by the sun. My anxiety always manages to creep its way in, a few pre-ride worry thoughts of what happens if you get sunstroke, what happens if your bike breaks, if you or Kyle get hit by a car, if you get lost, all possibilities of what could go wrong entered my mind, but once I was riding, alongside Kyle, I felt safe. The first day was the best day because, despite the period issues, it was my least painful day. The ride started with a motorbike lead out, keeping the group at a maximum pace of nineteen mph for the first six and half miles and as soon as the bike left, people went off like it was the Tour De France; I knew I couldn't keep that pace up for twelve hundred km so we let ourselves be pulled along by the group for a little while and then peeled off and stuck to our own pace, not wanting to burn our matches too soon. It was still dark and as we looked ahead on the long, straight road, there were red bike lights as far as the eye could see, some in clusters, some solo beams, hundreds of lives that had all come together for this one event, for this one shared passion. Some may say we are all crazy for choosing to ride this length; others may say we are inspirational, but really, we're just people riding our bikes; anyone could do it if they really wanted to. The sun soon came up and with that, the French summer heat hit us. At one of the control points, I stuck my head straight under the water tap and boy, did it feel amazing; I'd been craving coldness for the past fifty miles. We saw so many cyclists from all over the world; I rode with people from Toronto, Ireland, local Leicester, Poland and India. We saw one guy in a bright pink jersey and every time we passed him, or he passed us, I decided to call him 'pink panther'. it became a little motivator on the ride, 'when will we see pink panther again?', the most random sayings and ideas happen on long distance rides.

By midnight, we had done our first four hundred km and decided to sleep for three and a half hours; we got our sleeping and bivvy bags out on some grass by a church (not in the graveyard; that would have been too creepy). I looked up and WOW, I had never seen stars like it before, pitch black sky, bursting with white lights as far as I could see, from left to right, forward and back; it looked unreal. That is a memory that will stick with me forever, feeling so tiny in the world underneath the vast sky full of stars, but at the same time feeling, for the first time in a long time, as if I belonged; I didn't feel different from the people around me that I had met today, I didn't feel awkward or out of place, I felt at home around cyclists, like I was with extended family who I could be my complete and authentic self around, I could talk rubbish and no one cared, I felt like I was exactly where I needed to be, I felt no pressure to do anything at this moment other than be under the stars and I felt excited for the eight hundred km we had left to ride. If only I could bottle this feeling up and take it in doses when life gets too much or little irrelevant things start to cause unnecessary stress. I'm definitely going to take myself back to being under the stars in my mind next time I feel the anxiety brewing.

Three thirty a.m. marked the morning and the start of the next four hundred km; today, we would reach Brest and the halfway mark of the ride. When we started cycling, my heel/shin started to hurt and my bum was feeling a little uncomfortable; I knew we were in for a long day, but I whacked the chamois cream on my derriere and told myself there was nothing I could do other than keep riding. I didn't think it could get any hotter, but somehow it did; we climbed up La Roc, the biggest climb of the ride and were greeted at the top by locals playing out music and offering water. We freewheeled down into Brest, six hundred km in our loins, six hundred fourteen km to go. Two baguettes and stamps were collected at the control point and off we went again, waving and shouting "*merci*" as we rode past numerous French cheerleaders in little French villages, holding out water bottles, doing Mexican waves, smiles that radiated energy into my legs. We saw a little corner shop that seemed to have attracted lots of other cyclists, two of whom Kyle had met on his six hundred qualifier; with the temptation of ice creams, we stopped for two magnums, a very cute cat sat by us on the pavement, sneaking some crumbs in. We made a quick trip to the pharmacy that was conveniently opposite the shop for some painkillers (by this point, the heel was hurting every pedal and saddle sores had started to hurt a lot). We had a pep talk of encouragement from a fellow rider who told us that, in the end, we would be itching to do it again and that we'd soon forget about any pain we were in now. I was struggling to sit on the saddle by this point, but I loved the chats with other riders, the atmosphere of support and the long, smooth French roads; there was no way I wasn't going to finish this ride, so off we rode towards the next control, with a pack of fig rolls in my jersey pocket and the cool taste of white chocolate ice cream in my mouth. Darkness soon came back around and at eight hundred km in, we got another bit of sleep, again outside a church, but this time on concrete rather than grass; I was that tired I didn't notice and drifted straight off into a deep slumber, abruptly awoken by the three fifteen a.m. alarm.

Three-thirty a.m. morning again, pitch black sky, clouds hid the stars this morning and off we rode into the final four hundred km. This last part of the ride is a blur of pain; the final four hundred km took us a lot longer than the first two, mainly because I had to keep stopping and getting off the bike to deal with the pain in my shin (which turned out to be an irritated Achilles tendon I found out after the ride) and my bum. But the pain is mixed with happy memories of the sunrise at seven a.m., singing songs with made-up lyrics about bikes to keep going, "give me oil on my chain keep me spinning", a massive pizza, thinking 'blooming heck, I don't know if I can make it'. The last five hours were excruciating to sit on the saddle;

I had managed to get cuts in places you don't want to; the only positive was that it distracted me from the pain of my Achilles, which no longer hurt as much. At one point, we put Kyles's puffer jacket down my bib-shorts to try and give me some comfort, but then my feet couldn't reach the pedals, so it was yanked back out, a few tears were shed and I reminded myself that I had been through, so much worse in my head, some cuts on my fru aren't stopping me from finishing and the puffer jacket story does make us laugh now. The final control before the end was in a place called Druex, cycling in darkness; the long straight roads seemed never-ending, with red lights ahead. I had deja vu from the start, but this time, the lights moved a lot slower and we didn't catch many up. The only focus was to finish; it didn't matter how long it took. Just before the final control, we came into a little village where we heard loud voices and saw a glow of lights; my eyes lit up when I saw a little pub on the corner; it was filled with cyclists who were drinking coffees and eating pastries, all sat outside on little wooden tables. "Kyle, we're stopping!" Kyle didn't need me to say; he had already decided we were stopping, too. I've never seen him unclip from the pedals so fast! Two hot chocolates and two apple slices, I walked towards our table outside and my wrist decided to fail on me; hot chocolate went all over the floor with a massive crash, causing a sea of helmets to turn our way and an outburst of laughter as I just stood looking down at the puddle of yumminess dribbling towards the road. Surprisingly, the mug didn't break and the French waiter ran out and immediately filled us with another mug, a big smile on his face as he handed it to me and waved me away as I tried to pay again. The hot chocolates were so good, with French hot drinks being about a quarter of the size of ones in the UK, we ordered another each, enjoyed the taste and the sugar that gave us some more energy and rode off again, the sugar and short rest from the saddle giving us a much-needed boost. As soon as we got on the bikes, I started crying; the pain was starting to get unbearable and every turn of the pedal felt like the cuts were getting deeper, but with only thirty-five miles left in total, I reminded myself it was only a club ride to do, a ride I do on weeknights after work, nothing compared the how far we had cycled up to now. I put more chamois cream on, perched on the tip of my saddle, tried sitting on the top tube, cycling with only one bum cheek on the saddle and cycling off the saddle, but that hurt my heel too much. In all honestly, those last thirty-six miles were not enjoyable; it was just a case of gritting my teeth and telling myself, "You can do this. Don't give up, think of the end feeling, you can do; don't give up on the end feeling" over and over it went in my head. We put some music on and that was a great distraction for about half an hour; then the tears started again, Kyle encouraging me along. We reached Dreux, the final control point before the end and they were serving omelettes, Kyle's favourite; we had one each, the biggest pile of omelette I've ever seen and psyched ourselves up for the final twenty-six miles. I was in a world of pain, but I was also in a world of awe at the cyclists around me. We were in what looked like a big sports hall, tables laid out like we were at school dinner and all around, cyclists lay on benches fast asleep; some had their helmets down with heads in their hands and others were tucking into food like Kyle and me, all had a glazed look about them, but a smile spread easily from one cyclist to the other and sometimes that's all you need, a little smile, a look of, "we can do this". It was at this control that we saw Chris, one of the men we had travelled here with from our cycling club; he looked pretty tired out, but seeing a familiar face gave us all a bit more motivation to finish; we planned to ride the last bit together but in the commotion of the control point where lots of cyclists in the same PBP high vis blur into one and the dark making it hard to see who was who, we missed him as he left, reunited at the finish line where he told us he'd stopped for a quick ten minute nap in someone's garden before the end, unable to keep his eyes open.

So off we set for the final twenty-six miles, onto a pitch-black road with no street lights; all you could see was what your bike light lit up ahead and the stars above your head. Kyle started to imagine there were bears on the side of the road and we kept speaking to each other, checking we were safe and not too sleepy to keep riding. As we reached the last ten miles, I'd never been so close to giving up. The pain was unreal, but I said to myself, "Pain is just a feeling; it's my body's way of telling me that something isn't okay, but we are nearly done and then everything will be okay. Pain is just a feeling." I looked up and I saw a shooting star, the first I'd ever seen and it was heading towards the finish. It gave me the last little glimmer of hope I needed to get to the end and fuelled the fire within me to finish; pedal by pedal, I chased the shooting star and we eventually reached a Rambouillet sign. I shouted out in relief. "Whoooohooooooo!" Kyle let out an "Ohhhh yeeaaaaaa!" Freewheeling down, a smile started to emerge and relief started to spread through my body, "Kyle, we're going to do it!" Into Rambouillet, we freewheeled and onto a little gravel path towards the Chateau where we had started exactly three days ago, we bumbled over the gravel, dodging little stones, each bump adding the pain of the saddle. It was 5.33 a.m. seventy-two hours and three minutes had passed, one thousand two hundred nineteen km had been ridden and a million memories had been made. We rolled over the bump of the electric checker that tracked our time from the chip in the numbers on our bikes and rode under the blow-up arch that marked the end of the ride. I don't know how I felt reaching the end; I was so tired and glad to be back that I didn't really feel. I hardly had the energy to hug Kyle and say well done. We were both full of pride for each other and we ambled to the finisher's tent for our "finishers meal" with a PBP medal and a fully stamped brevet card in our hands.

I did Paris–Brest–Paris for anyone who feels like they can't; I did it to prove to myself that I'm not a failure; I did it to prove that I can get through hard things without giving up, I did it because I wanted to, I did it to show that no matter how hard life gets or how painful, it's worth keeping going because things always get better, pain always comes to an end. There was a time when I didn't think life was worth living, but I carried on living it and if I didn't, I wouldn't have got to experience this epic ride. Yes, there was pain, but the good moments outshone the bad moments by a million miles. Don't let the moments of pain in life stop you from living, dreaming and hoping.

Pain, like everything, including life, is temporary, so don't give up hope through the hard moments, push through the painful ones, live deeply in the happy times when they come around. Give out love and let yourself be loved. Cheer on the people around you, as well as being your own cheerleader. Welcome challenge with open arms and bask in your achievements without feeling afraid to celebrate what you're proud of yourself for. Most importantly, live life to the full; you have one life, so make the most of every day and remember that your mindset is everything; the way you think about something is so powerful, so don't let self-doubt stop you from living your life and achieving your aims.

Little mental health tip: Remind yourself that one day, you will look back on your life and think about what you want it to look like. There are things we can't control; let them go, but the things you can control, control them, steer your life towards happiness.

Finding Happiness

When I started this book, I was still struggling a lot. Writing helped me to make a tiny bit of sense of what was going on inside my head. I never in a million years expected this book to be published. It was on the second night of PBP, settling into my sleeping bag on the rock-hard concrete, that I checked my emails (as you do when you've ridden eight hundred km and it's one am); there was an email from the publisher (Kyle had encouraged me to send what I'd written into a few places, I was convinced it would have no chance of even being read past the first page). The email was offering me a publishing contract; I thought I must be dreaming or hallucinating from lack of sleep and didn't allow myself to get excited; surely this wasn't happening. But after getting home from PBP, pinching myself and checking the email multiple times, as well as getting Kyle to check, I realised this was actually happening.

There have been numerous times I've thought about deleting parts of what I've written, worried about what people will think of me and embarrassed about what I've been through in my mind. But it's also been very therapeutic to write and I wanted to share what I have to help anyone who's struggled or is struggling right now know that you're not alone, things can get better and happiness can be found again.

Even when low times or anxious times come, the happier times outweigh them all. I'm so grateful to have found cycling and I really don't know where I'd be without it. But it doesn't have to be cycling; it can be anything that makes your soul shine and gives you a sense of purpose and belonging. One thing I know is that whatever life throws at me, I'll never give up. There are lots more cycling adventures to come and I'll be riding for as long as my legs or, should I say, my cod loins let me.

Happiness is hard to define; it's a feeling and a feeling is a feeling; you can't touch it, but you can see it; you can often tell if someone is happy or sad by simple expressions and sometimes you can see it in their eyes. Happiness has the power to radiate from one person to another with a smile. It might only last a second, but one smile from me to you is a second of happiness shared. I've come to learn that aiming to be happy all the time isn't realistic; it's not here all the time, it's not permanent. But that's okay because it is the absence of happiness that makes happiness feel even better when it comes back. I've learned to accept that hard times come, but I know that they pass. I've found happiness in the small things, like feeling the warmth of the sun, smelling cinnamon from drinking a chai latte and in the big things, like having a mind free from intrusive thoughts or going on a long bike ride. As long as you have something to live for; family, friends, dogs, animals, cycling, weekends, the list can go on and you remind yourself not to take life too seriously, then you're on the right path to happiness. We all have lots of things to live for; we just have to let ourselves see them, recognise them and keep reminding ourselves of them. One day, we won't be here any more, so live your life. You can't rewind, but you can make a change to live happier, to think happier, to be happier.

I'll continue to search for ways to find happiness in life and look for ways to be at peace in my mind because there's still a way for me to go. Mental health isn't something that stays the same throughout life. On the down days that continue to surface every now and again, I will remind myself of the better days and I will never lose hope.

When I feel alone,
The bike brings a sense of home.

It's when I ride,
That my soul can truly shine.

Printed in Great Britain
by Amazon